Civil War Battles

AN ILLUSTRATED ENCYCLOPEDIA

★

The Civil War Society

Civil War Battles

AN ILLUSTRATED ENCYCLOPEDIA

The Civil War Society

GRAMERCY BOOKS

New York

Copyright © 1997 by The Philip Lief Group, Inc.

This 1999 edition is published by Gramercy Books,™
an imprint of Random House Value Publishing, Inc.,
201 East 50th Street, New York, New York 10022
by arrangement with The Philip Lief Group, Inc.,
130 Wall Street, Princeton, NJ 08540.

Gramercy Books™ and colophon are trademarks of
Random House Value Publishing, Inc.

Random House
New York • Toronto • London • Sydney • Auckland
http://www.randomhouse.com/

Printed and bound in the United States of America

Photographs courtesy of the National Archives and the Library of Congress

Designed by Helene Wald Berinsky

Library of Congress Cataloging–in–Publication Data

Civil War Society's encyclopedia of the Civil War. Selections
Civil War battles : an illustrated encyclopedia / the Civil War Society.
p.   cm.
"Originally published in a larger edition entitled The Civil War
Society's encyclopedia of the Civil War"—T.p. verso.
ISBN 0-517-20292-1
1. United States—History—Civil War, 1861-1865—Campaigns—Encyclopedias.
2. United States—History—Civil War, 1861-1865—Campaigns—Pictorial works.
I. Civil War Society.   II. Title.
E470.1.C6   1999
973.7'03—dc21   98-33254
CIP

Originally published and excerpted from) in a larger edition entitled
The Civil War Society's Encyclopedia of the Civil War (1997)

8 7 6 5 4 3 2 1

Civil War Battles

AN ILLUSTRATED ENCYCLOPEDIA

★

The Civil War Society

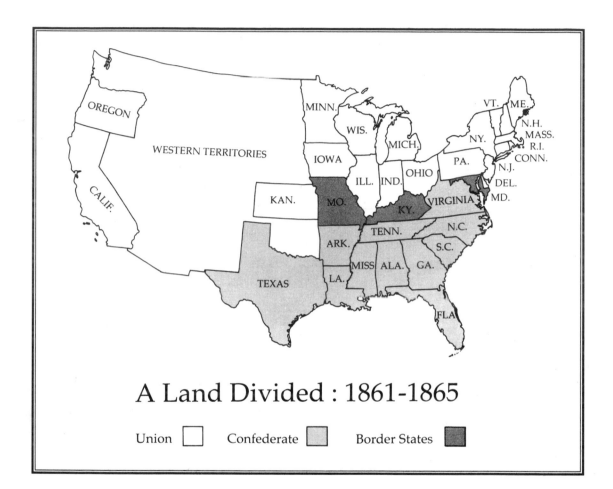

A Land Divided : 1861-1865

Union ☐   Confederate ☐   Border States ■

Antietam, Campaign and Battle of

SEPTEMBER 17, 1862

Determined to build upon the Confederate victory at Second Bull Run, General Robert E. Lee invaded the North through western Maryland, only to lose a decisive battle during the single bloodiest day of the Civil War. Combined Confederate and Union losses totaled more than 27,000 in just 12 hours of battle.

A major turning point in the war, the Union victory gave Abraham Lincoln the confidence to enact the Emancipation Proclamation, thereby changing the war's aims from sustaining the Union to pursuing the more lofty goal of human freedom and increasing Union troops by including black soldiers. In addition to consolidating a series of Confederate wins during the spring and summer (including a victory in Kentucky by Braxton Bragg, which allowed Lee to open a second front in the eastern theater), Lee had many reasons for invading the North at this time: to relieve an exhausted Virginia from further ravages of war, at least temporarily; to attract support and recruits from Maryland, a border state with strong pro-Confederate sentiments; and, perhaps, to win a decisive victory that could force a Union surrender.

Lee's ultimate goal was the capture of the Federal rail center at Harrisburg, Pennsyl-vania. To reach it, he devised a campaign which he outlined in Special Order No. 191. The campaign called for the division of his Army of Northern Virginia. While Lee moved his troops into Pennsylvania, Major General Thomas J. "Stonewall" Jackson would capture the Union garrison at Harpers Ferry, then join Major General James Longstreet's three divisions, and together they would move forward until they met up with Lee near Harrisburg. Although Union troops far outnumbered the Confederates, Lee's bold plan may have succeeded because Union commander George McClellan, uncertain of both the strength and the whereabouts of Lee's forces, hesitated to move against them.

By a cruel twist of fate, however, a Union corporal made a discovery that changed the course of the campaign and, hence, the course of the entire war. On September 13, he found a copy of Special Order No. 191 wrapped around three cigars in a meadow near a former Confederate camp, which he immediately forwarded to McClellan. Although the general now had his enemy's strategy in his hand, McClellan continued to display his customary caution. Afraid that the document was a trap and that the 40,000 Confederates actually outnumbered his more than 95,000 troops, McClellan refused to take action for over 16 hours.

In the meantime, Lee, who learned within 24 hours that his plans had been conveyed to the enemy, did his best to shore up his three

Felled Confederate soldiers at Antietam.

vulnerable flanks: his lone division at South Mountain; two divisions that were with Longstreet a few miles north at Hagerstown; and Jackson's troops, more than 30 miles south heading toward Harpers Ferry. Fighting soon broke out in several locations, including Fox's Gap, Turner's Gap, and Crampton's Gap, resulting in heavy Confederate losses. On the morning of September 15, Lee was preparing a retreat to Virginia when he learned that Jackson had captured Harpers Ferry, garnering valuable supplies. Instead of retreating, he ordered all of his divisions to converge at the town of Sharpesburg.

Once again hesitating when action was necessary, McClellan allowed this to occur, waiting until the morning of September 17 to attack. The long day of battle began at 6 a.m., with 75,000 Union troops facing Lee's diminished force of just 40,000. Lee's left flank, located in the woods around a 40-acre field, was hit first and hardest. In places with serenely pastoral names such as Dunker Church, the Cornfield and the West Woods, Confederate troops were decimated by wave after wave of Union troops led by Joseph Hooker, Joseph Mansfield, and Edwin V. Sumner. Only when two fresh Confederate divisions joined Jackson's troops was the Federal attack on the left flank halted—in just 20 minutes, more than 2,200 Yankees were wounded or killed in the West Woods—and Sumner forced to retreat. By the middle of the day, the Union turned its attention to crushing the Confederate center, led by Major General Daniel H. Hill, which converged along a sunken lane.

Sumner's remaining two divisions stormed Hill's line for three hours; the battle resulted in so much mayhem the narrow street was forever after known as Bloody Lane. The Confederate center was now broken. Union forces under Ambrose Burnside crossed Antietam Creek to attack Lee's right flank in mid-afternoon. The Confederate army might have been completely destroyed then and there had not A.P. Hill's division arrived from its 30-mile march from Harpers Ferry in time to deliver a crushing counterattack.

Despite heavy Confederate losses, Lee did not retreat immediately, nor did McClellan take the upper hand and crush his enemy. Instead, the two leaders, who watched almost equal numbers of their men fall during the day, allowed their troops to rest for 24 hours. On the evening of September 18, Lee withdrew into Virginia, about a quarter of his troops having been killed or wounded in the action at Antietam.

★ ★ ★

Appomattox Station, Cavalry Fight at
APRIL 8, 1865

In the ongoing attempt to bleed dry the Army of Northern Virginia in the Appomattox Campaign, in the closing days of the war in Virginia, Union General Philip Sheridan sent General G. A. Custer to try and take advantage of unguarded openings in Robert E. Lee's lines, left as a result of fighting the previous day at Farmville, Virginia, a few miles up the Appomattox River. It was Custer's job to keep Lee from reuniting his scattered forces, by moving west and then north of Lee's position and attempting to block him into the neighborhood of the county courthouse. In a wire to Abraham Lincoln, Sheridan said "if the thing is pressed, I think that Lee will surrender." Lincoln then wired Ulysses S. Grant, quoting the cavalryman and adding the injunction: "Let the 'thing' be pressed." As Custer moved in and captured Lee's vitally needed supply trains at Appomattox Station, the Second, Fifth and Sixth Corps of the Union Army maneuvered, with support from the Army of the James, to surround Lee's men. The way to Lynchburg, the only escape route Lee had been able to see, was now blocked; Lee sent a courier to Grant asking to discuss not necessarily surrender terms per se, but simply to ask "the terms of your proposition." That night, with Grant's response in hand, Lee held his final council of war with his commanders, deciding they would attempt one last assault the next morn-

The site of formal Confederate surrender at Appomattox Court House.

ing, which was Palm Sunday—April 9, 1865. That attack was never launched, however, as Lee realized the futility of such a tactic; he instead arranged to surrender his army to Grant at Appomattox Court House.

Army, Confederate

Because there was so much confusion and destruction in the South during the waning days of the Confederacy and the months following the surrender of the various armies of the South, facts and figures concerning the makeup of the Confederate military organization are often hard to come by. Records show-

ing interesting minute details of the average Confederate soldier either do not exist any longer, or have yet to come to light. We know that by the war's end many of the survivors had enlisted at comparatively younger ages than their Union opponents, or comparatively older ages; the population of the South was considerably smaller than that of the North, and there were fewer men of appropriate battlefield age available to fill in the ranks when death, disease, and wounds thinned out the lines of battle. But we do not have their averages of height, weight, occupation, or level of education. Some fragmentary records show that the officers were generally elected from among middle-class and upper-class men with prior military experience, either from the Old Army of before the war, or from attending the numerous military schools that were always popular in the South. The Confederate soldier was slightly more rural in background than the Yankee; many more of them had been farmers, and fewer of them lived in cities. New Orleans and Baltimore were the only cities in the Old South that even approached the sprawling size of Northern cities like Boston, New York, Philadelphia, and Cincinnati. On the average, it can be presumed the Confederate soldier in the ranks was slightly less well educated than the Union boys; in the balance, however, there were better riders and marksmen in the ranks of the South than in the North, for these were soldiers who hunted to live, and who rode from an early age.

There were fewer recent immigrants in the Southern army, as well. Most of these men were of Scots/Irish, English, Welsh, African-American, Cherokee, or Hispanic descent, and could point to ancestors who had been in their region since the colonial days and earlier. They had the advantage, right from the start, of familiarity with the ground on which they fought; their cause, too, was perhaps more clearly cut. They were not necessarily fighting to preserve slavery; the majority of Confederate soldiers had never owned a slave in their lives. They were fighting to save their homes and families, fighting for the right of their states to self-government. They were suspicious of the invading Yankees, and truly believed, at least at first, that the Northern folks were evil people who wished to destroy them. They soon learned that there was very little difference between themselves and the average Northerner, however, and there was a great deal of visiting, trading, and chatting between the two armies when they were not shooting at one another. Perhaps the most

Robert E. Lee's soldiers in Virginia, 1864.

telling argument concerning the reason a Confederate lad entered the army was uttered when a Northern soldier asked a captured Southerner why he was fighting, only to be told: "Because you're down here!"

The Confederate army had more to lose than the armies of the Union, and over the course of the four-year war most of their fears in that regard were true. Robert E. Lee, in particular, had strict rules and regulations forbidding his soldiers to prey on civilians when in Union territory. Union soldiers in battle and sometimes while merely encamped, did great damage to the South. They burned private homes, destroyed fields and forests, and set fire to courthouses with their irreplaceable records—all in the name of punishing Southerners, who they believed to be traitors. When the war was over, many a Confederate came home to find his family destitute, their home gone, their farms all but unusable. It was hard to claim one's land anew when the records of tax surveys were gone, and the Confederate currency had been so devalued by inflation during the war that the majority of Confederate citizens were hard-pressed to rebuild.

Confederate soldiers, often outnumbered by their Union counterparts, fought with great determination. They were very often barefoot, wearing threadbare uniforms and subsisting on hardtack, unbolted cornmeal, and water. The Army of Tennessee, the Army of the Carolinas, the Army of Georgia all made valiant contributions to the Confederate cause, but, perhaps because of the fame of their commander, the peerless Robert E. Lee, the Confederate army most people remember best is the Army of Northern Virginia. More books and articles have been written about this army than about perhaps anything else in Confederate history.

Army, Union

The Union Army, according to the best estimates based on careful review of figures from 1861 to 1865, consisted of approximately two million, two hundred thousand men, ranging in age from roughly 18 to 46, the average age being in the mid-twenties. Statistics have been compiled which give an interesting picture of the common Union soldier. The majority of them had never been in military service before, and most of them had been farmers before the war broke out. Their average height was around five foot eight; the average weight was just under 145 pounds. Slightly over three-quarters of the boys in blue had been born in America, and were mostly volunteers; the drafts held at various times during the war only added about six percent to the total force in the field.

Their reasons for fighting were almost as varied as the soldiers themselves. Some enlisted to free the slaves, while others joined up because their friends went, or in pursuit of excitement. Many of them became soldiers because they felt the Union had to be preserved, and that it was their duty to bring that about. And some, in common with young men of all times and places, went because it was the right thing to do—or out of fear of being labeled a coward for staying home.

Meticulously equipped and poorly trained, they were at first at a great disadvantage on the field of battle. They were, after all, the invaders; they did not know the territory into which they were marching. They headed south believing in their cause, but knowing that the rumor mill gave most of the points to the Confederates: it was widely believed that the South had better commanders at all levels, better cavalry, and better training. Some of this was actually true, and when battlefield experience backed up rumors, the game of war lost a great deal of its glamour.

Their leaders eventually figured out what they were doing, or were dismissed for lack of results; after a virtual parade of failures or might-have-beens in command of their armies, the remaining generals were some of the best soldiers the North had left: Philip Sheridan, John Buford, Winfield Scott Hancock, George Henry Thomas, William Tecumseh Sherman, and Ulysses S. Grant. Under these men and numerous talented others, backed by a seemingly endless supply line and a greater population from which to draw more soldiers when death thinned the ranks, the men of the Union army finally prevailed over the ill-equipped and depleted Southern armies.

In campaigns such as Gettysburg, Fredericksburg, Atlanta, Vicksburg, the Seven

The New York 7th Regiment, leaving for the front.

Days, the Peninsula, and many more, the Union soldier learned his lessons and sought every weak point he could in Confederate defenses. The many armies under the banner of the Union were named after major rivers in their area of operation: the Army of the James, which fought in southern Virginia and North Carolina; the Army of the Tennessee, not to be confused with the Confederate Army of Tennessee (the state), which besieged Vicksburg and fought Albert Johnston in Tennessee and Kentucky; the Army of the Mississippi, the Ohio, and of the Cumberland. Perhaps the best known of the Union Armies, however, was the Army of the Potomac, led by several prominent generals, of whom Grant was ultimately the most effective. A less well known fact is that army names, or nomenclature, could be decidedly confusing; the Army of the Potomac began the war as the Army of Virginia, which was exactly the same name as the army the Federals met when they invaded the South! The Union changed its army to Potomac— and the Confederates changed theirs to the Army of Northern Virginia.

Atlanta, Campaign and Siege of

MAY 1–SEPTEMBER 2, 1864

For four months in the summer of 1864, outnumbered and out-supplied Confederate troops fought hard—but finally failed—to keep their supply lines open and the Union from capturing Atlanta, Georgia. Ultimately a decisive Union victory, the Atlanta campaign resulted in an equal number of casualties—about 30,000—on each side.

Driven from Tennessee during the Chattanooga Campaign, 62,000 Confederates now under Joseph E. Johnston amassed at Dalton, Georgia. Facing them were approximately 100,000 Federal troops, led by Major General William T. Sherman. While Ulysses S. Grant's drive for Richmond and Petersburg continued in the east, Sherman's objective in the west was clear: to cut all rail lines leading to and from Atlanta and, finally, to take the city itself. Known as the "Gate City of the South," Atlanta was the Confederacy's second most important manufacturing and communications center. Johnston, knowing that his forces were not strong enough to defeat Sherman outright, tried instead to keep him from reaching Atlanta for as long as possible—hopefully until after the November election. Without a convincing victory at either Richmond or Atlanta, the war-weary North might deny Abraham Lincoln's reelection, thereby giving the Confederacy a chance to negotiate with a more sympathetic Union president. Unfortunately for the Confederate cause, Johnston's plan was ultimately rejected.

At the beginning of May, however, Johnston remained in command of forces securely entrenched along Rocky Face Ridge, a sheer rock wall surrounding a canyon through which both the highway and the railroad to Chattanooga passed. The ridge's lower six miles formed the east wall of the Snake

Ripping tracks in preparation for the evacuation of Atlanta.

Creek Gap, where one of the first skirmishes between Union Major General James B. McPherson's division and Johnston's troops fought. McPherson was forced to fall back, allowing the Confederates to retreat further south. Sherman pursued and another battle occurred at Resaca from May 14–15. For more than five weeks of often vicious fighting at places such as New Hope Church, Mount Zion Church, Picketts' Mill, and Pine Mountain (where Confederate Lieutenant General Leonidas Polk was killed), Johnston was forced to drop down to Kennesaw Mountain. Setting up defensive positions along the mountain's steep, rocky slopes, he was able to repulse Sherman's frontal assault on June 27. Confederate rifle and cannon fire felled more than 2,000 Union men, compared with just 500 Confederate losses.

Nevertheless, by July 4, Johnston had been pushed down to within seven miles of Atlanta. When he withdrew south of the Chattahoochee River, removing the last natural barrier between Sherman and Atlanta, Confederate president Jefferson Davis—anxious for more decisive and aggressive action—

replaced Johnston with Major General John B. Hood. Hood quickly delivered the action Davis wanted. Using a plan devised by Johnston, Hood saw an opportunity to strike Sherman's army, which had been divided at Peachtree Creek, on July 20. Although the Confederate infantry troops fought valiantly, the attack ultimately failed, 4,800 Rebels were lost, and Hood retreated to Atlanta.

Thinking that Hood was abandoning the city altogether, Sherman sent McPherson to the south and east of Atlanta in pursuit. Hoping to surprise McPherson, William Hardee's infantry division launched the ill-fated Battle of Atlanta on July 22, losing more than 8,500 men. At 3,700 casualties, the Union experienced a lighter loss, but the respected and able James McPherson was killed there. Sherman continued his advance by sending McPherson's replacement, Major General Oliver Howard, around the western side of Atlanta to cut off Hood's communications line to the south. Hood launched a third attack at Ezra Church on July 28. Able to protect the railroad, Hood nonetheless lost another 2,500 men. The Confederate army, depleted to less than 45,000, fell back behind Atlanta's formidable defensive lines and waited for Sherman to attack. Sherman instead laid seige. Bringing up heavy Federal artillery, he began a bombardment that would last for more than a month while, at the same time, he attempted to completely seal off the city's supply lines. Thanks in large part to the skill of Confederate cavalry commander Joseph E. Wheeler, the Rebels were able to keep the Union from crushing their supply route until the end of August.

On August 28, however, Sherman struck at the Montgomery & Atlanta Railroad south of the city; desperate to keep this vital rail line open, Hood attacked the Union flank at Jonesborough. His loss there decided the outcome of the long siege of Atlanta. The Confederates evacuated the city on September 2; the next day Federal troops marched in. Once a grand manufacturing city, Atlanta lay in ruins, decimated not only by Union shelling, but by the retreating Confederates, who set tremendous fires and looted the city's remaining stores and supplies, preferring to destroy Atlanta's resources rather than see them fall into enemy hands.

Brandy Station, Battle of
JUNE 9, 1863

The biggest cavalry engagement of the Civil War, this battle proved that the Union's mounted troops could be a match to the seemingly invincible horsemen of the South. Army of the Potomac commander Joseph Hooker, suspecting that Robert E. Lee's Army of Northern Virginia was planning a major offensive, ordered Alfred Pleasonton, his new cavalry leader, to conduct a reconnaissance mission across the Rappahannock River. In fact, Lee was preparing for an invasion of Pennsylvania, with Jeb Stuart, commander of the cavalry corps that was the army's eyes and ears, concentrating his force of 10,000 by the river at Brandy Station to cover the Confederate advance.

The 114th Pennsylvania Infantry at Brandy Station.

Stuart took time out, however, to present a grand review of his brigades before a thrilled audience of civilians, highlighted by a flashy simulated cavalry charge. Reprising the show when Lee arrived on June 7, Stuart delayed his preparations for the imminent offensive. Meanwhile, Pleasonton's forces, more than 11,000 strong, commenced their mission on June 8. At dawn the following day, hidden by heavy morning fog, the Union cavalry crossed the Rappahannock and took Stuart's forces completely by surprise.

Over the next hours, more than 21,000 troops from the two sides engaged in a mammoth, classic hand-to-hand cavalry battle—the largest that would ever be fought on the North American continent—with headlong charges by saber-, pistol-, and rifle-wielding horsemen accompanied by the sound of artillery fire and bugle calls. The initially scattered Confederate force rallied and mounted a strong counterassault that pushed the Union cavalry back. Near sundown, when Pleasonton spotted Rebel infantry reinforcements marching toward the field, he ordered a calm withdrawal back across the river. The Union force suffered 936 casualties, 486 of whom were captured, while Stuart's troops lost 523. Because he held the field, the Confederate cavalry leader claimed a victory.

But Pleasonton accomplished his goal, reporting back to Hooker that Lee's army was indeed massed and ready to move north. As importantly, the aggressive Union general demonstrated that his cavalry was no longer the maligned, appearance-obsessed body far inferior to the Confederacy's splendid mounted troops; indeed, it was now a powerfully effective scouting and fighting force. Acknowledging that fact, the Southern press and public ridiculed Stuart for being caught off-guard at Brandy Station and focusing more on showing itself off than supporting Lee. "If he is to be the 'eyes and ears of the army,'" a Richmond newspaper criticized, "we would advise him to see more and be seen less."

Humiliated by the episode and anxious to redeem his reputation, Stuart embarked with his best brigades on attention-getting raids later in the month. While the forays won his renewed acclaim, they did Stuart's commanding general as much harm as good. Out of touch with his scouting force at this critical juncture, Lee would have little idea of the strength or whereabouts of the enemy as he launched his fateful invasion of the North.

Bull Run (First), Campaign and Battle of
JULY 16–21, 1861

The first battle of the Civil War, fought on both sides by inexperienced and ill-prepared troops, ended in a surprising victory for the South.

The Civil War began on this summer day not because of any military imperative, but because of several political and popular considerations. Convinced of a quick and easy win for their side, both Confederate and Union civilians were eager for the war to begin. In the South, people claimed that one Confederate could easily whip five Yankees; Northerners believed that their superior moral resolve, combined with formidable industrial resources, would win the day. Another source of pressure was the Confederate intention to have its Congress meet in the new capital of Richmond, Virginia, at the end of July; Northern politicians insisted that action be taken to prevent such treason, coining the slogan "Forward to Richmond!" The North had another especially compelling reason to begin battle at this time: the majority of its troops had signed up for three months of service just after the fall of Fort Sumter in April, and their enlistment terms were about to expire.

Military commanders on both sides, however, agreed on one point: their armies were not prepared for battle. Winfield Scott, the Union general-in-chief, proposed a plan involving a minimum of military action but a maximum amount of time. This plan was reluctantly overruled by Abraham Lincoln, who bowed to public pressure. Ordered by their commanders-in-chief, Union General Irvin McDowell and Confederate General Pierre T. Beauregard began to map their war strategies in early July. McDowell's goal was to invade Virginia, crush the Confederate forces, and move "forward to Richmond" to reclaim the capital. It was up to Beauregard to stop

New Union volunteers just prior to First Bull Run.

him and, with any luck, so impress the Union with Confederate strength that a truce would be called and the Confederacy allowed to exist. The Union forces in Virginia consisted of about 49,000 men; the Confederates numbered about 35,000.

Each side was divided into three armies: McDowell's 30,600 troops along the Potomac faced Beauregard's 20,000 Confederates, who amassed behind a creek called Bull Run near the vital rail line at Manassas Junction; near Harpers Ferry, Union General Robert Patterson's 18,000 men faced 12,000 Confed-

erates under Joseph E. Johnston; and Yankee Benjamin Butler, who commanded about 10,000 men, occupied Fort Monroe at the tip of the Virginia peninsula and was guarded by a small contingent of Confederates led by John B. Magruder. (Neither Butler nor Magruder would play a part at Bull Run.) McDowell's immediate objective involved attacking Beauregard and driving him from Manassas. He proposed to do this by first feigning an attack on the Confederate center then coming down hard on the Confederate left.

Coincidently, Beauregard had a similar flank movement in mind. Attacking McDowell's troops when they least expected it, he would then swing his right flank and strike the Union left. Crucial to McDowell's plan, however, was his advantage in numbers. For this to hold, he needed to keep Johnston from joining the battle. Ordering Patterson to keep Johnston occupied at Harpers Ferry, McDowell left Washington on July 16, heading for Manassas Junction. Patterson, however, was not up to the task, and the wily Johnston was able to slip away. McDowell's army moved very slowly—too slowly, it might be said—and did not make contact with the enemy until July 18, when Union soldiers on a reconnaissance mission were driven back by Confederates at Blackburn's Ford—a preliminary victory that greatly encouraged the Southerners.

Finally, on July 21, the battle began in earnest. Beauregard's plan, based on Napoleon's strategy at Austerlitz, failed almost immediately, due to his troops' inexperience. McDowell's men were equally green, but because they outnumbered their enemy, they gained an early upper hand. A number of Confederate units were overpowered as Union infantry advanced on a small plateau called Henry House Hill. It was here that Brigadier General Thomas J. Jackson, who commanded a Virginia division, was given his now famous nickname. Standing resolutely before the Union onslaught, he inspired one of his colleagues, Brigadier General Barnard Bee, to exclaim, "There is Jackson standing like a wall." This was just the first of many battles advanced by Stonewall Jackson's skill and bravery.

Just when it seemed as if the optimistic "Forward to Richmond" might be possible, Johnston's troops arrived from Harpers Ferry. Attacking with vigor, they forced the Union line to fall. When the retreat was called, the men who just days ago set out from Washington with such high hopes were now made to rush to the rear under fire. To add insult to injury, their retreat was hampered by the presence of hundreds of sightseers from Washington who had arrived in carriages and buggies to watch the action from a grassy slope a few miles away. Expecting to see an easy win for the Union, they received firsthand knowledge of the bitter bloodshed to come. In many ways, the First Battle of Bull Run foreshadowed the course of the entire war: the South, outnumbered and lacking supplies, fought bravely and cleverly, despite the odds; the Northern command moved slowly and with considerable indecision, giving precious time to the enemy. The victory—this time for the South—was won at too high a cost in human lives, even for the victor. The Federal losses at First Bull Run numbered 2,968 men killed, wounded, and missing; Confederate losses amounted to 1,982.

★　★　★

A view of the desolate battlefield at Bull Run.

Bull Run (Second), Campaign and Battle of

AUGUST 26–SEPTEMBER 1, 1862

Fought over approximately the same territory as First Bull Run just over a year before, Second Bull Run came to roughly the same end as well. Although vastly outnumbered, the South pulled off an extraordinary victory, largely due to its superior leadership and organization. After experiencing the exhausting and draining battle of the Seven Days campaign of the month before, both armies in the East spent the month of July resting, reorganizing, and planning their next offenses. Although the Confederates had protected Richmond during George B. McClellan's Peninsula campaign and during the Seven Days battles, they had gained no new ground. Major General Robert E. Lee, urged by some of his most able and respected generals—including Thomas "Stonewall" Jackson—was planning a bold offensive northward, hoping at least to move the action from the James River to north of the Rappahannock.

The North, still reeling from its failure, fundamentally reorganized its eastern forces. Major General George McClellan's army remained at Harrison's Landing, Virginia, and refused to forge another assault unless given substantial new recruitments. His continued stubborn resistance to action forced Abraham Lincoln to look for other leaders who would advance the Union's position. He summoned Major General Henry W. Halleck from the West in mid-July to become the general-in-chief of all Federal forces. In addition, he ordered Major General John Pope from the Western theater, where he had distinguished himself at Corinth, to command the newly formed Army of Virginia, giving him primary responsibility for launching another attack on Richmond as soon as possible.

Attempting to instill discipline in his troops, Pope made a mistake all too common in the North's high command: he insulted the integrity of the volunteer army and disparaged the entire army's previous performance, thus engendering resentment from his troops and offending his commanders. Pope's forces were divided at the beginning of August: 75,000 men were located on the north side of the Rappahannock River, while McClellan's 90,000 lay to the east on the Peninsula.

Lee's goal was to keep Pope and McClellan's forces from uniting and overwhelming his own 55,000 men. He developed a bold plan, which involved dividing his troops in two, sending Thomas "Stonewall" Jackson with 24,000 to capture the high Union supply depot at Manassas Junction. He and Major General James Longstreet would follow the next day with 30,000 men to meet Jackson at Manassas. After learning of Jackson's capture of Manassas, he sent his troops to find and destroy the wily general, but could not locate him or his troops for more than a day; Jackson had quietly left the garrison and amassed his troops on the battlefield of First Bull Run.

In the meantime, Pope, partly due to his poor relationship with his field commanders, lost track of Lee and Longstreet's division, who were rapidly approaching. Pope and Jackson clashed in a brutal two-day battle from August 28 to 30. The Southerners repulsed attack after attack by the right half of the Union army. Exhausted at the end of the day, Jackson pulled back some of his troops.

Pope mistook this retrenchment for retreat, sending word to Washington that the enemy was about to retreat and that he was prepared to pursue. Unknown to Pope, however, Lee and Longstreet had reunited with Jackson on August 29, bringing 30,000 fresh troops into the fray. When Pope set out to cut off the supposed retreat, the Confederate forces were ready for him. The entire Union line crumbled under the assault and retreated. Although troops from McClellan's Army of the Potomac arrived on August 31, it was too late. Pope was forced to withdraw into Washington. The Southern victory at Second Bull Run was a costly one for both sides: the casualties from August 16 to September 2 totaled about 14,500 men.

★   ★   ★

Carolinas Campaign
1865

Undeterred by miserable weather and nearly impassable terrain, William Tecumseh Sherman's grueling and ruthless winter 1865 advance through South and North Carolina was a far greater logistical triumph—and an even more destructive enterprise—than his notorious "March to the Sea." Shortly before Christmas, the Union force arrived in Savannah, Georgia, after completing its devastating trek through the state. Sherman was then ordered to turn north and bring his troops up to Virginia, where he would join Ulysses S. Grant to wipe out Robert E. Lee's forces and finish the war. Slicing through the Carolinas, a region left largely unscathed by the conflict, the Northerners would cut the Confederate army off from the Southern heartland and ravage anything in their path that the enemy could use to continue fighting. Due to the worst winter rains in two decades and other problems, the campaign did not commence until February 1.

Once underway, however, Sherman's 60,000-man army could not be stopped. With little military opposition to offer, the Confederates assumed that the elements

Columbia, the captured capital of South Carolina.

would scuttle—or at least bog down—the Union troops' advance. The swampy tidewater region that Sherman's army traversed was arduous terrain in even the best conditions, with dozens of rivers and tributaries fraught with alligators and snakes. The rains so flooded the area that Sherman's advance patrols often had to scout by canoe. But the Union army included experienced backwoodsmen and thousands of veterans who had become accustomed to difficult marches in their years of Civil War combat.

From the thick forests around them, they fashioned miles of log pathways called "corduroy roads" along the swamped route, built bridges and causeways, and, when necessary, waded up to their shoulders through the icy streams. Nursing hatred toward South Carolina—the birthplace of the secession movement—the Federal troops took special delight in their invasion of the state, and as they reached populated areas many engaged in indiscriminate looting and burning of civilian property, worse than their pillaging in Georgia. Sherman cut through the center of the state toward the capital of Columbia.

Left weakly defended, the town was occupied on February 17, and, within a day, almost completely destroyed by fire. Southerners claimed Sherman's drunken soldiers purposely set the blaze, but the Union general claimed that retreating Confederate forces tried to burn bales of cotton and other supplies in their hasty departure. As Columbia smoldered, Union troops proceeded to Charleston—the home of Fort Sumter—which was ransacked but left standing.

Four days later, on February 22, Federal forces under John Schofield captured Wilmington, North Carolina, the South's last open Atlantic seaport. The same day, deciding that the Union army had to be confronted, Robert E. Lee returned Joseph E. Johnston to command. Having faced Sherman before during the Atlanta campaign, the Confederate general did what he could to prepare for another showdown, gathering a force of 20,000 with help from stalwart cavalryman Wade Hampton, whom Lee had sent down from Virginia.

But Johnston was certain little could stop the Union army, the likes of which, he said, the world had not seen "since the days of Julius Caesar." Entering North Carolina on March 7, Sherman's troops curtailed their plundering but continued to move north, occupying Fayetteville on March 11. Five days later, Johnston was ready to challenge them, fighting a vigorous delaying action at Averasboro, then sending his whole force to attack the Union left wing under Major General Henry W. Slocum near Bentonville on the nineteenth. By the third day of what would be one of the final Civil War battles in the East, the entire Federal army, outnumbering the Confederates three-to-one, poised for assault, and Johnston was forced to withdraw. Having covered an extraordinary 425 miles in 50 days, Sherman's men arrived in Goldsboro on March 23, joining with John Schofield's forces and bringing the total number of Union troops marching northward to over 80,000. By the time the Federals reached Raleigh on April 13, Johnston had received word that Robert E. Lee had surrendered, and though Jefferson Davis ordered

The 3rd Pennsylvania Cavalry, March 1864.

him to continue fighting, he knew it was pointless.

The next day, Johnston called for a truce, and an armistice agreement was signed on April 18. After some squabbling among the Union high command over Sherman's authority to choose the terms, Johnston formally surrendered on April 26, essentially ending, aside for some lingering resistance in the West, the Civil War.

Cavalry, Confederate and Union

Although cavalrymen theoretically fight from the saddle, almost all cavalry corps in the Civil War were "dragoons" or mounted infantrymen: they rode to battles on horseback, but dismounted to fight. The Confederate army had two major cavalry corps which, at least for the first two years of the war, were better equipped and better trained than their Northern counterparts. Confederate Major General Joseph Wheeler's cavalry corps was part of the Army of Tennessee. Comprising Wheeler's corps were 4,200 horsemen, who distinguished themselves in several battles in the western theater, including Murfreesboro and the extraordinary maneuvering at Chattanooga known as Wheeler's Raids.

In the east, the Army of Northern Virginia's cavalrymen, famous both North and South for their abilities and showmanship, were led by Jeb Stuart. Stuart was promoted to brigadier general and given command of all the army's cavalry after his victory at First Bull Run. His cavalry corps grew steadily and performed well during the first two years of the war, generally out-riding and out-fighting their Union counterparts, particularly during the Seven Days campaign. At the beginning of the war, the Union had just one cavalry corps attached to its Army of the Potomac.

Early in the war, a number of volunteer cavalry regiments were called in to supplement the infantry, but until the spring of 1863, when Joseph E. Hooker took command of the corps, mounted soldiers were poorly trained and used. Once organized and trained, however, the Union cavalry distinguished itself in battles such as Brandy Station (the first and only true cavalry battle of the Civil War) and Gettysburg.

In April 1864, Philip H. Sheriden took command of the cavalry corps, which now numbered nearly 12,500 men. Sheriden was able to lead his corps to victory at Five Forks on April 1, 1865, a battle which broke open the defenses of Petersburg and led to Lee's surrender at Appomattox Court House. The cavalry in the Union's western theater was not organized into a corps until the end of November, 1864, but then played a decisive role in the Battle of Nashville and in Sherman's March to the Sea.

★   ★   ★

Chancellorsville, Battle of
APRIL–MAY 1863

Called "Lee's masterpiece," this Confederate victory allowed the South to take the initiative in the eastern theater in the spring of 1863. Facing a force more than double his own, Robert E. Lee skillfully, and with nerves of steel, outmaneuvered his less decisive opponent, Joseph E. Hooker, and drove him north of the Rappahannock River.

After a discouraging winter of defeats in Fredericksburg and during Ambrose E. Burnside's "Mud March," Abraham Lincoln replaced the inept Burnside with "Fighting Joe" Hooker. The cocky Hooker had distinguished himself in the Peninsula Campaign and at Antietam and was a vocal critic of Burnside. When he took control of the Army of the Potomac, he did so with vigor, inspiring the troops with an energy and confidence his predecessor lacked—and an arrogance that would prove his downfall. "May God have mercy on General Lee, for I will have none," he wrote to Lincoln on the eve of a planned offensive against Robert E. Lee's troops centered around Fredericksburg. Leaving a third of his 115,000 troops near Fredericksburg to keep Lee occupied, he led the other 75,000 men on a long swing up and across the Rappahannock and Rapidan to strike at Lee's unprotected left flank and rear.

On April 27, Hooker arrived at Chancellorsville, a house in the midst of a clearing ten miles west of Fredericksburg, and set up camp, certain that he would destroy Lee's army within 48 hours. His plan may have worked had he not faced a man far more clever and audacious than he. With just 60,000 troops, Lee used the same plan that had met with such success at Second Bull Run a year before: he divided his troops. Leaving just 10,000 men at Fredericksburg, he rushed the rest west to shore up his flank. The first clash occurred on May 1 when Hooker's men headed south toward Confederate lines.

Trudging through woods so dense they were called the wilderness, the men were surprised by an attack led by Thomas "Stonewall" Jackson. Hooker, who later admitted that he simply lost his nerve, ignored the advice of his corp commanders and ordered a sudden withdrawal back into the Wilderness. When Lee's cavalry commander, Major General Jeb Stuart, reported that Hooker's right flank was vulnerable, Lee took another huge risk and further divided his forces to take the offensive. He ordered Jackson to march with 26,000 men beyond Hooker's vulnerable flank and attack while he remained with troops at Chancellorsville.

Although alerted to Jackson's movements by his scouts, Hooker was not convinced Jackson posed any real danger. Troops under General Oliver O. Howard were relaxing in camp when Jackson swooped down upon them at twilight on May 2, forcing them to withdraw some two miles to the rear before Union artillery stopped the Confederate sweep short of the Chancellorsville house.

In the midst of this great victory, the Confederates sustained a deadly blow when Jackson was shot inadvertently by his own men in the growing darkness. Stuart took command of the infantry, and at daylight on May 3 launched another assault on Hooker's lines, pushing them back to the Rappahannock and Rapidan. Meanwhile, Lee's rear was threatened by Union troops advancing under the command of Major General John Sedgwick.

On May 4, a detachment from Lee's forces at Fredericksburg swarmed the Union contingent at Salem Church, fighting a vicious daylong battle, until Sedgwick finally withdrew across the Rappahannock at nightfall. The next day, Hooker's army joined the retreat in what was—considering its overwhelming advantage in manpower—one of the most needless and humiliating Union defeats of the war. His boasts of a great victory ended in more than 17,000 Union casualties.

Hooker was removed from command of the Army of the Potomac about a month later. Lee's victory, however, was in many ways a Pyrrhic one. Not only did he lose almost 13,000 soldiers—a greater percentage than did the Federals—he also lost Stonewall Jackson, one of the South's greatest and most irreplaceable assets.

Chattanooga, Campaign and Battle of
OCTOBER–NOVEMBER 1863

The battle over the gateway to the eastern Confederacy and the rebel war industries in Georgia was long and fierce, but it ended with Tennessee firmly in the Union's hands. Under siege by Major General Braxton Bragg since their humiliating defeat at Chickamauga the month before, Union troops in Chattanooga were cold, hungry, and discouraged.

At the beginning of October, Bragg sent his cavalry corps commander, Joseph Wheeler, out on a series of raids that effectively cut off all Union supply lines. The arrival of Major General Ulysses S. Grant, just appointed commander of the newly formed Military Division of the Mississippi, signaled the start of a new Union offensive. Replacing William S. Rosecrans with Major General George H. Thomas as commander of the Army of the Cumberland, Grant and his chief engineer, William F. Smith, devised a bold plan to break the siege. The first order of business involved opening a supply line by assaulting the Confederates on the east bank of the Tennessee River, then setting up a bridgehead at Brown's Ferry. Supplies shipped by water to Brown's Ferry could then be hauled across Moccasin Point to the hungry troops in Chattanooga.

After driving the Confederates off Raccoon Mountain, the Union put its "Cracker Line Operation" into effect on October 26. Although the Confederates assaulted the new line at Wauhatchie from October 28 to 29, the first steamboat laden with Union supplies arrived safely on November 1. While waiting for reinforcements to come from Memphis and Vicksburg with Major General William T. Sherman Grant planned the next phase of his offensive: to drive the Confederates off their perch on

Missionary Ridge, along the north- and southeastern side of Chattanooga and from Lookout Mountain on the southwest.

Meanwhile, the Confederates underwent profound—and unwise—organizational changes. Braxton Bragg, a man disliked and disrespected by virtually everyone who knew him, experienced a quasi-mutiny of his corps commanders. Lieutenant General Leonidas Polk, Daniel H. Hill, and Thomas C. Hindman asked for and were granted transfers by the War Department after they complained about Bragg's indecisive and slow actions at Chattanooga. Bragg also ordered several divisions and 35 cannon under Lieutenant General James Longstreet eastward to aid West Virginia troops in their actions against Ambrose Burnside, weakening his lines on Missionary Ridge just as the Federals were planning to attack.

On November 23, news of Sherman's arrival with fresh troops allowed Grant to proceed. His first objective was to take Orchard Knob, the Confederate's forward position in the center of their line on Missionary Ridge. The battle began when divisions dressed as if for a military parade marched below the hill. When bored and curious Confederates on the knob came down for a closer look, Union troops rushed them and, after a pitched battle, took the hill. Making Orchard Hill his headquarters for the fight, Grant then ordered Sherman's divisions, located north and west of Chattanooga, to cross the Tennessee River and attack the Confederate right on the north end of Missionary Ridge.

In the meantime, Hooker's goal was to

take Lookout Mountain on the Confederate left. Moving forward at 4 a.m. on November 24, Hooker found himself embroiled in a blind battle with the enemy. Sheets of rain and dense fog hid most of the battle from the troops below, earning the fight for Lookout Mountain the nickname "Battle above the Clouds." When the fog cleared, however, the Union flag flew from the crest. While Hooker had been enveloping the Confederate left, Sherman had been slogging his way through the rain to Bragg's right, not arriving until the afternoon of November 24.

Bragg then made a fatal mistake. He split his forces, putting half on the bottom of the hill with orders to fire a volley when the enemy got within 200 yards, then withdraw up the slopes. Hampered by his usual lack of communication skills, Bragg failed to fully inform all the men of this plan. The next morning, the Battle of Missionary Ridge began.

Sherman's troops and artillery battered Confederates along the north end, but were repulsed several times. To draw Rebels away from Sherman's front, Grant ordered Thomas to attack the Confederate line at the base of the ridge. Although some of Bragg's men knew enough to withdraw immediately, most stayed and fought—and died, overwhelmed by Union troops. After taking the line, the men—without orders from either Grant or Thomas—decided to pay back the Rebels for their humiliating loss at Chickamauga. They went straight up the steep mountain slope and drove the Confederate army off in complete retreat.

The defeat at Chattanooga was a severe blow to an already weakening Confederate cause. The loss of the vital communication and supply lines that ran through the city made Sherman's Atlanta Campaign possible.

Chickamauga, Battle of
SEPTEMBER 19–21, 1863

The Confederate army came close to delivering a knockout blow to Federal forces in the West in this horrific two-day September 1863 battle, the region's deadliest Civil War confrontation. After a nearly bloodless campaign ending earlier in the month, Union commander William Rosecrans' Army of the Cumberland occupied Chattanooga, Tennessee, strategic gateway to the southeastern Confederacy.

Eager to continue pressing Braxton Bragg's Army of Tennessee, Rosecrans listened to false rumors fostered by Bragg that the Southern troops were retreating and launched his forces in pursuit. Actually, the Confederate general was gathering reinforcements in northern Georgia to mount an attempt to retake Chattanooga. With the arrival of James Longstreet's corps, his force now outnumbered Rosecrans', 60,000 to 50,000.

Moreover, the Union army had to separate into three columns during its advance through the hilly terrain below the city. Delays and poor coordination kept Bragg's subordinates from successfully attacking the scattered Federals, however, and the clashes alerted Rosecrans to Bragg's ruse. On September 13, the Union general was able to start regrouping his troops, assembling by the

The battle lines at Chickamauga, Georgia.

west bank of Chickamauga Creek, a small stream just across the Georgia border. Union and Confederate patrols skirmished near the creek on September 18, and the battle began in earnest the following morning.

Bragg's new goal was to attack Rosecrans' left flank and destroy the whole Union army by forcing it into a dead-end valley to cut off any possible retreat back to Chattanooga. Onslaughts by entire divisions of Southern troops were met by counterassaults from George Henry Thomas' corps in a day of brutal, hand-to-hand combat amid dense woods that concluded with only minimal Con-

federate gains and heavy losses on both sides. After Leonidas Polk delayed a sideways echelon attack against Thomas early on September 20, Bragg ordered Longstreet to launch an all-out frontal assault. The Confederate commander's timing could not have been better. Rosecrans, unable to spot a large section of his troops obscured by the thick forest, mistakenly believed there was a breach in his line and sent a whole division to fill it, creating a real gap on the Union right in the process. Longstreet's forces smashed straight through, overrunning the Union commander's headquarters and sweeping nearly one half of his army from the field. With Rosecrans himself among the troops sent reeling back to Chattanooga, George Henry Thomas was left in command of what remained of the Federal force. Refusing to retreat, he rallied the troops to form a stalwart, if tattered, line on the ridge of Snodgrass Hill. Relentless assaults by Longstreet and Polk's men throughout the rest of the day failed to dislodge the forces under Thomas, who would earn himself a celebrated nickname, "The Rock of Chickamauga."

Finally, at dusk, he ordered a withdrawal. The Confederates won a huge victory, although Thomas' legendary stand saved the Union army from annihilation. Both sides suffered devastating casualties: 16,000 for the Union and 18,500 for the Confederacy— nearly 30 percent of the troops involved in the battle. Among the dead were a teenaged girl who had disguised herself as a soldier to fight for the Union, and Confederate Brigadier General Ben Hardin Helm, brother-in-law of Mary Lincoln and a close friend of the president. Ten of Bragg's generals had been either killed or wounded, and his despondency over the heavy cost of victory kept him from following up the next day with an attack on the Federal forces still in retreat. Bragg's surviving subordinates were furious that he let the Union army return unchallenged to their solid Chattanooga fortifications. Longstreet and Polk wanted Bragg to be dismissed and Nathan Bedford Forrest refused to serve under him any longer, while the Confederate commander suspended Polk and two other generals for what he claimed were inferior battlefield performances.

Despite the bickering and the lack of a conclusive blow against the Union army, the victory at Chickamauga raised spirits throughout the South, which had been demoralized by two big losses earlier that summer at Gettysburg and Vicksburg. With the Army of the Cumberland pinned at Chattanooga and about to be besieged by Confederate forces, the North's hopes of holding onto eastern Tennessee were now tenuous.

Cold Harbor, Battle of
JUNE 3, 1864

Culminating the awful one-month campaign in Virginia that had already seen the Battles of the Wilderness and Spotsylvania, this contest was Robert E. Lee's last major field victory and, by his own admission, probably the worst mistake of Ulysses S. Grant's Civil War career. After the fighting at Spotsylvania concluded, the two commanders followed what was becoming a familiar routine, the Union Army of the Potomac advancing further south toward Richmond to try to get around Lee's Army of Northern Virginia and provoke a clash, and the Southern forces dashing ahead to entrench themselves and await the coming onslaught.

There were few lulls in the fighting: in late May, the opponents battled along the North Anna River and Totopotomoy Creek. Both armies then lurched toward Cold Harbor, a crossroads hamlet near the Chickahominy River that was little more than a single tavern, only eight miles from

Part of General Grant's army crossed this pontoon bridge during the Battle of Cold Harbor.

the Confederate capital. Again, the Southerners got there first, a cavalry unit under Lee's nephew Fitzhugh approaching on May 31 and confronting Philip H. Sheridan's mounted troops.

The Union managed to seize the crossroads and held on during a seesaw battle among arriving infantry forces the following day. Replenished with fresh troops, the Union and Confederate armies alike, despite their grievous losses during the month's fighting, were as large as they had been at the start of the campaign: 110,000 and 60,000 strong, respectively. Although the North had a far greater supply of manpower, most of those sent to Cold Harbor had seen little action, while the Southern reinforcements were experienced battle veterans.

Still, believing the enemy was thoroughly exhausted and dispirited, Grant began to see his chance for the knockout blow against the Confederates that he had been waiting to deliver. "Lee's army is really whipped," the Union commander was convinced, suspecting that a successful assault at Cold Harbor could destroy the Southern force altogether and might win the war right there. Grant ordered Winfield Scott Hancock's corps, which performed so well at Spotsylvania but was not yet on the field, to lead a massive attack he scheduled for the morning of June 2. Marching all night, they were delayed by heat and fatigue, and Grant had to postpone the assault until dawn the next day. The holdup allowed Lee's army to dig in and form a virtually impregnable seven-mile line, protected on both ends by two rising rivers, as the Confederate commander nursed an illness.

With Grant planning an all-out attack against the forbidding Southern defenses, it was his troops, not Lee's, who were demoralized that evening, many pinning pieces of paper with their name and address to their uniforms so that their bodies could later be identified. At 4:30 a.m. on June 3, the Federal assault began, a force of more than 50,000 rushing straight toward the enemy. The entrenched Confederates, hidden by the terrain, waited until the hapless foe got close, then, with a thunderous sound, let loose devastating barrages of gunfire. Unit by unit, the advancing Union men were simply mowed down. Nearly 7,000 fell in the first minutes of the charge. "It was not war," Confederate general Evander Law would later remember. "It was murder."

Although some in Hancock's corps had been able to breach a section of Lee's line, they were quickly repulsed. Within 30 minutes, it was all over—a total failure. Grant called off the attack, ordered his troops to begin digging trenches for a prolonged stay, and assessed the damage. The entire battle had cost him over 12,500 casualties, while Lee's losses were under 4,000. "I have always regretted that the last assault on Cold Harbor was ever made," the Union commander wrote later.

Unwilling to admit defeat to his enemy, it would be days before he would ask for a truce to collect the wounded men still left on the field. By the time a ceasefire was arranged, almost all of them had died. The two forces remained entrenched at Cold Harbor until the evening of June 12, when Grant ordered a withdrawal in the darkness. The war in Virginia then took a new turn as the Union troops headed south yet again—to begin an assault on Petersburg.

Crater, Battle of the
JULY 30, 1864

With the potential of being a spectacular success, this mine assault against the Confederate defenses at Petersburg, Virginia, instead became one of the Union army's most tragic fiascos. By June 1864, Grant and his generals were looking for a way to break the entrenched Confederate line protecting the strategically vital Virginia town. Members of a regiment of Pennsylvania coal miners stationed at the front had an idea of their own.

The aftermath of the explosions on July 30, 1864 (Battle of the Crater).

By running a mine shaft, packed with explosives, underneath a temporary Confederate stronghold built on high ground 150 yards away, they could simply blow up the fort and watch as a few divisions moved right through the Rebels' center and into Petersburg.

A colonel in the regiment, Henry Pleasants, a mining engineer himself, thought the idea was an excellent one, and brought it to the attention of his corps commander, Ambrose Burnside. Recognizing the chance to salvage his blemished war record in a single, sensational act, Burnside approved the plan,

despite the skepticism of his superiors George Meade and Ulysses S. Grant. The Pennsylvania regiment began digging the tunnel on June 25 under Pleasants' supervision, receiving no help from sneering army engineers. Resorting to makeshift tools and using Pleasants' improvised ventilation system, they spent the next month successfully constructing—undetected, contrary to most expectations—a shaft 511 feet long, ending 20 feet directly under the Confederate line.

Up top, Burnside began planning the assault. He assigned his one fresh division to

lead the attack, black soldiers who received special training and were eager to prove themselves capable of front-line assignments.
Whether he doubted their abilities or feared
negative public reaction, Meade overruled
Burnside, ordering him to choose a white division to lead the chancy assault instead. Shortly
before 5 a.m. on July 30, a charge of four tons
of gunpowder packed in the mine shaft exploded in a phenomenal blast, making a crater 170
feet long, 70 feet wide, and 30 feet deep.

Several Confederate units were flung into
the sky, one entire regiment and an artillery
battery were instantly buried, and Southern
soldiers for hundreds of yards around ran in
terror.

But the federal assault did not begin for one
hour. The commander of the ill-prepared division now leading the attack, James H. Ledlie,
was busy drinking rum in a shelter while his
troops advanced. Moving forward with two
other divisions, many of the soldiers jumped
down into the hole rather than going around it.
By this time, the Confederates had regrouped
and surrounded the rim of the crater, shooting
down on the Union troops trapped inside who
made gruesomely easy targets. Avoiding the
crater, the black division, meanwhile, met a
strong Confederate counterattack.

As was all-too-frequent, scores of the black
soldiers were shot by infuriated Southern
troops while trying to surrender. The total
casualties for the Union were 3,798, while the
Confederates lost approximately 1,500.
Calling the failure "the saddest affair I have
ever witnessed in the war," Grant dismissed
James Ledlie and gave an extended leave to
Burnside.

Five Forks, Battle of
APRIL 1, 1865

The campaign which would culminate in
the surrender of Lee's Army of Northern
Virginia began at this confluence of five major
roads above Petersburg, Virginia, with a decisive clash between Confederates George
Pickett, Fitzhugh Lee, and W.H.F. "Rooney"
Lee, versus the cavalry of Union General
Philip Sheridan and Gouverneur K. Warren's
5th Corps of Infantry. Pickett had orders from
Robert E. Lee to "hold Five Forks at all haz-
ards," since the crossroads was on the far right
of Lee's army, and Ulysses S. Grant had begun
a systematic process of extenuating Lee's line
to the point of desperate thinness by constantly moving left, forcing the Confederates
to counter or be flanked. Pickett ordered his
men to dig in, and the two younger Lees
probed throughout the morning and early
afternoon to try and keep constant watch on
the progress of Sheridan's pickets.

The situation was tense and difficult on
both sides; Warren and Sheridan were busy
accusing each other of improper conduct and
failure to move fast enough or to support
where ordered, and one of Fitz Lee's junior
officers, General Thomas Rosser, invited
Pickett and Fitz Lee to a shad bake some miles
from where their men were busy containing
the enemy. With inattention the order of the
day on both sides, by late afternoon the situation was ripe for disaster.

Sheridan sent forth dismounted cavalry
directly at the Confederate front, while
Warren got his infantry into motion and

attacked to the left. Rooney Lee, technically in command of the cavalry forces because his cousin was absent from the field, had not been apprised of Fitz Lee's departure—and thus did not know he had twice as many troops of which to make use. Pickett's second in command was equally unaware of his commander's absence, to similar disastrous effect.

Inexplicably, at the height of the battle with success in full view, Sheridan sent to Grant for permission to relieve Warren of command for being slow, disobeying orders, and lack of cooperation, charges from which Warren was later exonerated—too late to save his reputation or career. The end effect of the fight at Five Forks was that Pickett's men had been quite effectively separated from the main army—crippling Lee's line to a dangerous degree.

Fort Donelson, Battle of
FEBRUARY 13–16, 1862

In order to take control of Kentucky and western Tennessee, Union commander

The Battle of Fort Donelson.

Ulysses S. Grant devised a plan to capture Fort Donelson, a Confederate garrison located 12 miles east of Fort Henry, which had fallen into Union hands a few days before. Grant knew Fort Donelson would not be easy to take; it was manned by a force equal to his own (about 17,000 men). It was, however, commanded by two men for whom the general had little respect: Brigadier General John B. Floyd and Major General Gideon J. Pillow.

Grant planned to take Donelson by using his army to block the fort while Flag Officer Andrew H. Foote's gunboats shelled it into submission. On February 14, in the middle of the afternoon, Foote's ships steamed upriver. When they were just 400 yards from the fort, they began to fire, only to be met with a ferocious counterattack. With the guns on high ground above the river, however, the Confederates had the advantage. Within a few hours, two of six Union vessels were sunk, the rest badly damaged, and Foote himself wounded.

After this defeat, Grant assumed that the only way to take the fort would be through a long siege during the cold Tennessee winter. For reasons still unknown, however, Pillow and Floyd apparently believed the fort was indefensible and decided to evacuate on the morning of February 15. Planning to cut their way through the Union lines and open a road to Nashville, Confederate cavalry, under Nathan Bedford Forrest, attacked the Union's right flank in the snow- and ice-covered woods outside the garrison. Fighting bitterly for several hours, Forrest had just carved out an escape route when Pillow inexplicably ordered his men to fall back, leaving only a thin line of defense to hold the position.

Grant's fierce counterattack quickly regained the ground the Union had lost, pushing the Confederates back to the fort. As night fell, the Confederate commanders considered how and when to surrender. General Floyd demurred, claiming that he had sworn an oath never to surrender. Pillow, too, declined, leaving the sorry duty to the third in command, Simon Buckner. During the night, Floyd, Pillow, and some 2,500 men escaped by boat, and Forrest's mounted infantrymen rode across the frozen Cumberland backwater. Buckner, meanwhile, sent a note to Grant, asking surrender terms. He received a reply that set the standard for the war: "No terms except an unconditional and immediate surrender can be accepted." On the morning of February 16, 15,000 men surrendered to the Federals. Both the Tennessee and Cumberland rivers were now in Union hands.

Fort Henry, Capture of
FEBRUARY 6, 1862

A gunboat flotilla commanded by Flag Officer Andrew H. Foote subdued this Confederate fort, located at the crucial juncture of the Tennessee and Cumberland rivers.

Along with Fort Donelson, Fort Henry formed the linchpin of the Southern line of defense from Columbus to Bowling Green,

Kentucky, then southward to the Cumberland Gap. Its capture would ensure that both Kentucky and western Tennessee remained within the Union and give the Union armies an invasion route to the South.

Built on low ground near the edge of the Tennessee River, Fort Henry was not easily defensible—in fact, at the time of the attack, some of the fort was submerged under flood-level waters. This fact was not lost on its commander, Brigadier General Lloyd Tilghman, who decided to send most of his men to defend Fort Donelson. He kept just 100 artillerymen to fire the fort's 17 guns.

The Union forces, led by Brigadier General Ulysses S. Grant, numbered approximately 15,000. A naval force commanded by Foote consisted of three unarmed gunboats and four ironclad river gunboats, any one of which was powerful enough to subdue the enemy. Grant's strategy, reluctantly approved by his commander, Major General Henry W. Halleck, included a combined attack between his ground and naval forces. Action commenced on February 6, as Union gunboats came within 600 yards of the fort and fired.

By the time Grant's forces, delayed by muddy roads, arrived at the fort, all but four Confederate guns were destroyed, about 20 Confederates were killed or wounded and 63 were missing, and Tilghman had surrendered. Federal losses amounted to 11 killed, 5 missing, and 31 injured. The first step in the Union plan to invade the South completed, Grant's men regrouped at Fort Henry until the night of February 11, when they started their overland march to Fort Donelson.

Fort Pillow, Battle of
APRIL 12, 1864

"The river was dyed with the blood of the slaughtered for 200 yards," Nathan Bedford Forrest reported after the battle of Fort Pillow. "It is hoped that these facts will demonstrate to the Northern people that negro soldiers cannot cope with Southerners." One of the largest engagements between black soldiers and Confederate troops during the Civil War continues to engender controversy today.

Located in Tennessee about 40 miles north of Memphis on the east bank of the Mississippi, the Union's Fort Pillow was charged with protecting Federal navigation along the river. In April 1864, it was held by 262 black soldiers (the 11th U.S. Colored Troops and Battery and the 4th U.S. Colored Light Artillery) and 295 whites (the 13th Tennessee Calvary). These men were under the command of Major Lionel F. Booth, with Major William Bradford second in command, and were reinforced by Captain James Marshall's ironclad, the *New Era*.

On April 12, 1,500 Confederate troops under Nathan Bedford Forrest arrived at dawn prepared to take the fort. Confederates, perched atop the small hills that dotted the surrounding terrain, fired directly into the fort. One bullet hit and killed Major Booth at 9:00 a.m., leaving Bradford in command. At 11:00, Forrest ordered a general assault to take the fort's south barracks; with this accomplished, the Confederates were able to bombard the fort's interior with more small-arms fire. At 3:30, Forrest sent in a demand for sur-

Rebel massacre of Federal troops at Fort Pillow.

render. Bradford demurred, asking for an hour to decide. Forrest, realizing that Federal reinforcements were on their way, gave him just 20 minutes. Bradford's reply was succinct: "I will not surrender."

The Confederates then charged the fort and drove the Union troops down the riverbank, where they encountered another contingent of Confederate troops, under Captain Charles W. Anderson. At the end of the day, 230 Federals had been killed, 100 wounded, 168 whites and 58 blacks captured. How the casualties occurred, however, remains in dispute.

Federal accounts claim that Union troops surrendered as soon as the Confederates entered the fort, but were massacred in cold blood by soldiers shouting racial epithets, including "Kill the damn niggers. Shoot them down!" Southerners, on the other hand, insist that the losses were incurred because the Federals refused surrender and lost their lives fighting on the banks of the Mississippi.

The Joint Committee on the Conduct of the War conducted an investigation and issued a report of the incident, which included hair-raising accounts by Union troops of Confederate brutality. Whether or not the event amounted to wholesale slaughter, as the Union claimed, it appears likely that the Southern soldiers acted upon their deep animosity toward whites who tolerated black soldiers and, of course, toward the black soldiers themselves.

Fort Sumter
APRIL 12–13, 1861

Commencing on April 12, 1861, the two-day bombardment of the Union garrison at Charleston Harbor, South Carolina, signaled a bloodless start to the Civil War.

With the nascent Confederacy taking control of military installations throughout the South, the very visible Federal presence at the birthplace of secession was considered a particular affront. Despite South Carolina's demands in late 1860 that Union forces leave Charleston, two companies, numbering less than 100, resolutely remained stationed at Fort Moultrie under the command of Robert Anderson, a Kentucky ex-slaveowner with Southern sympathies but resolute Northern loyalties. Still, an indecisive President Buchanan offered no directives about how to deal with the hundreds of secessionist militia that had amassed in the city.

On December 26, Anderson took up a more secure position in the middle of the harbor at Fort Sumter, a formidable pentagon-shaped brick structure, whose construction,

begun in 1829, was still not complete. His situation remained precarious, with a belated reinforcement attempt failing in January, when Confederate gunfire kept the Union's relief ship *Star of the West* from entering the harbor.

By March, Anderson reported to incoming President Abraham Lincoln that, unless he received provisions, Sumter would fall within weeks. Though Union General-in-Chief Winfield Scott and most of Lincoln's cabinet favored abandoning the fort, public sentiment in the North demanded the stalwart garrison not be forsaken. The president, avoiding an overt act of aggression that might lose support for the Union, announced in early April that he would attempt peacefully to supply Sumter. Considering that provocation enough, Confederate President Jefferson Davis ordered Pierre G. T. Beauregard, commander of the 6,700-man force now ringing Charleston Harbor, to take the fort.

Hours before dawn on April 12, a handful of Southern officials rowed out to the fort to order its surrender. Anderson refused, and at 4:30 a.m., the Confederates commenced shelling. Hopelessly outgunned and outnumbered, the tiny Union force managed only sporadic return fire, while civilians lined the waterfront to view the bombardment. After 34 hours under assault, with several buildings ablaze inside the fort, the Federals capitulated and were allowed to return North.

Neither side suffered any casualties until the fighting ceased, when, in the middle of the surrendering garrison's hundred-gun salute to its lowered flag, a freak explosion killed two Union men. Rousing emotions in

Confederate flag flies over Fort Sumter after Union forces withdraw, April 1861.

North and South alike, the events at Charleston Harbor finally sparked the long-coming Civil War.

On April 15, Lincoln called for 75,000 volunteers to quell the "rebellion." Two days later, as the South also began mobilizing, Virginia voted to secede from the Union. The North would not regain Fort Sumter until Charleston was occupied in the conflict's final days. At a huge ceremony on the afternoon of April 14, 1865—five days after Lee's surrender and just hours before Lincoln's assassination—Robert Anderson brought out the battered American flag he had taken down from the beleaguered fortress exactly four years earlier and triumphantly raised it once again.

Franklin, Battle of
NOVEMBER 30, 1864

Hoping to reawaken the Army of Tennessee's fighting spirit with a brash frontal assault against the deeply entrenched enemy, Confederate John Bell Hood lost a quarter of his force in this battle.

The general's actions had been brazen since he took command four months before. Invading Tennessee after Atlanta fell to William T. Sherman's army, Hood had not only hoped to cut off the Union's supply line—halting its devastating march through Georgia—but even to drive all the way through Kentucky and come to Robert E.

Lee's rescue in Virginia with a rear attack on Ulysses S. Grant's forces.

The wildly ambitious campaign began in late November, when Hood's army of 40,000 entered Tennessee from Alabama. Sherman sent John Schofield with 30,000 men to reinforce an equal number of George Henry Thomas' troops at Nashville. The combined Union forces would likely be more than enough to thwart Hood, so it was the Confederate general's intention to keep them divided.

At first, he was successful in pursuing and outmaneuvering Schofield. After three days of fighting outside Columbia, Hood had the opportunity on November 29 to trap the Union force at the crossroads of Spring Hill. His poorly coordinated attempt to replicate Stonewall Jackson's brilliant Chancellorsville flanking maneuver failed, however, and the Federal troops were able to continue on their way to Nashville.

Reaching the town of Franklin, 15 miles south of the Tennessee capital, on the morning of November 30, the Union forces were unable to cross the damaged bridges spanning the Harpeth River. Schofield ordered his soldiers to erect fieldworks and dig in while the bridges were being repaired. By the time Hood and most of his army arrived on the scene shortly after noon, the Federals had formed a heavily fortified arched line protected on both ends by the river and an abundance of artillery.

The formidable defenses did not faze the Confederate commander, though. Blaming his failure at Spring Hill on his troops' timidity, Hood decided to force them to more

aggressive action: a headlong assault against the Union line. The attack had little strategic purpose—Schofield was clearly planning to withdraw soon anyway—and much of the Confederate force, including its artillery, was too far in the rear to be used.

Recognizing the debacle they faced, Hood's subordinates—including Nathan Bedford Forrest, a man who could hardly be accused of lacking gumption—vehemently opposed the plan, but their commander, more convinced than ever that they and their troops needed a good fight, went ahead. Without artillery cover, the attack began at 3:30 p.m., an extraordinary effort rivaling Pickett's Charge at Gettysburg. Union soldiers held their fire until two of their front-line brigades withdrew to safety, then let loose a furious barrage against the 20,000 advancing Confederates spread across nearly two miles of open ground.

Pressing forward even while they were being shot down by the hundreds, the Southern troops proved Hood had no reason to doubt their mettle. But their situation was hopeless. Sheer momentum carried some over the Union line, only to be trapped in the trenches they had just overrun. The Confederates launched several more desperate charges, and the fight continued in the dark until they finally pulled back at 9 p.m.

Two hours later, Schofield ordered a quick withdrawal as the Federal forces resumed their movement north to Nashville. The futile assault cost Hood's army more than 6,250 casualties, including 12 generals, while Union losses were under 2,400. With his numbers greatly depleted and his troops now seriously doubting the abilities of their commander, Hood's chances for success in Tennessee were dimmer than ever. Yet, the resolute Confederate still advanced his pummeled army toward the state capital, where it would face even larger and more daunting Union forces.

Fredericksburg, Campaign and Battle of
NOVEMBER–DECEMBER 1862

One of the Union's worst Civil War defeats, the Battle of Fredericksburg was a tragic demonstration that superior numbers could not make up for inferior generalship. Ambrose Burnside, who had reluctantly replaced the hesitant George McClellan as Army of the Potomac commander in November, promptly fell under pressure from both Abraham Lincoln and the Northern public to mount a new offensive against the Confederacy. Since Richmond remained the popular target, the accommodating general planned an immediate movement of his entire force of 120,000 toward the Southern capital by way of Fredericksburg. The initial advance was startlingly swift, as Union troops marched 40 miles east from their encampments near Warrenton Junction.

By November 19, Burnside's army had arrived across the Rappahannock River from Fredericksburg, to find the Virginia town lightly defended and Confederate commander Robert E. Lee unprepared for an assault.

Burnside could not attack, however, because he did not yet have the pontoons his huge army needed to bridge the river.

Bureaucratic blunders delayed their arrival six days, and even after receiving them, Burnside waited nearly another three weeks. By that time, Lee had concentrated his forces; Fredericksburg was evacuated and 75,000 solidly entrenched troops of the Army of Northern Virginia lined the hills overlooking the town. Though he had lost the advantage, Burnside refused to call off his planned offensive. To the contrary, he calculated—incredibly—that his best chance was to surprise Lee by a direct assault on the most formidable point of the Confederate line.

At dawn on December 11, Burnside finally ordered army engineers to begin constructing six pontoon bridges across the Rappahannock, their progress hindered by sniper fire. Lee, satisfied with his brilliantly formed defensive position, allowed the Federals to approach. By the next day, Burnside's troops had finished crossing the river and occupied Fredericksburg, spending the hours before battle on an unseemly looting spree.

The Union onslaught began at 9 a.m. on December 13, as William B. Franklin's corps advanced against the Confederate right, commanded by Stonewall Jackson. Leading two cannon out to the middle of the field, Southern horse artillery officer John Pelham faced down the entire attacking force, startling Lee and the Federals alike with his audacity. George Meade's division managed to breach the Confederate line, but had to fall back when they received no reserves. A Southern counterassault, in turn, was repelled

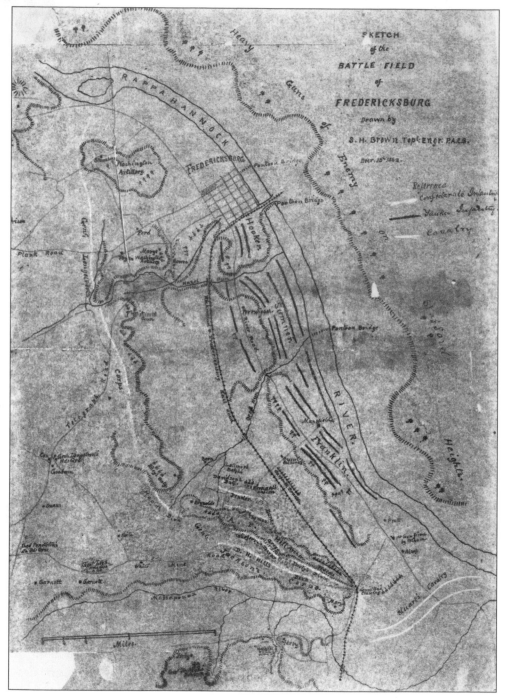

Map of the Battle of Fredericksburg.

by Union artillery fire, and the two sides continued to skirmish inconclusively as Franklin declined to resume his advance. "It is well that war is so terrible," Lee remarked, watching the battle. "We should grow too fond of it."

Meanwhile, Burnside launched his main thrust against James Longstreet's impregnable position at Marye's Heights. Atop the ridge, hundreds of Confederate guns aimed down on the sloping open field that the Federals were about to traverse, while four ranks of infantrymen waited along the sunken road at the base, protected by a 4-foot-high stone wall that ran more than half a mile. "A chicken could not live in that field once we open on it," a Confederate predicted, and that was hardly an exaggeration.

The charging Federals could not get near the stone wall before being annihilated by the almost nonstop fire pouring forth from behind it. Brigade after brigade streamed out of Fredericksburg in their valiant but hopeless attempts to storm Marye's Heights, as a seemingly oblivious Burnside continued ordering assaults through nightfall.

That evening, as the aurora borealis—rarely seen so far south—lit the winter sky, the distraught Union commander discussed renewing the offensive the following morning, planning to lead the charge himself. Talked out of the suicidal plan by his officers, Burnside withdrew the Northern army back across the Rappahannock during a heavy storm on the night of December 15.

Union casualties at the Battle of Fredericksburg exceeded 12,500, most cut down on the frozen fields approaching Marye's Heights, while the Confederate lost fewer than half that number—about 5,000. As well as destroying the Army of the Potomac's morale, the appalling defeat sobered spirits throughout the entire North during the bleak Christmas season of 1862.

Gettysburg, Battle of
JULY 1–3, 1863

This three-day victory for the North remains the epitome of the bloody tragedy that was the Civil War. The battle of Gettysburg, Pennsylvania, effectively ended the second, and final, Confederate invasion of the North.

Undertaken after Robert E. Lee's stunning victory at Chancellorsville, the risky invasion encompassed several Confederate priorities. First, Lee did not want another battle to take place in Virginia, where supplies were scarce and communities already savaged by months of war. Second, a battle won on Northern soil possibly could win the Confederacy some much-needed foreign support. Strangled by the Union blockade, overwhelmed by the North's superior manpower and matériel, the South desperately needed a stunning victory.

Believing that a best defense is a strong offense, Lee advanced the first of his 70,000 troops from Fredericksburg northwestward on June 3, 1863. Just four days later, the Battle of Brandy Station was fought between Union and Confederate cavalry near Culpeper, Virginia. Although the Rebels were able to

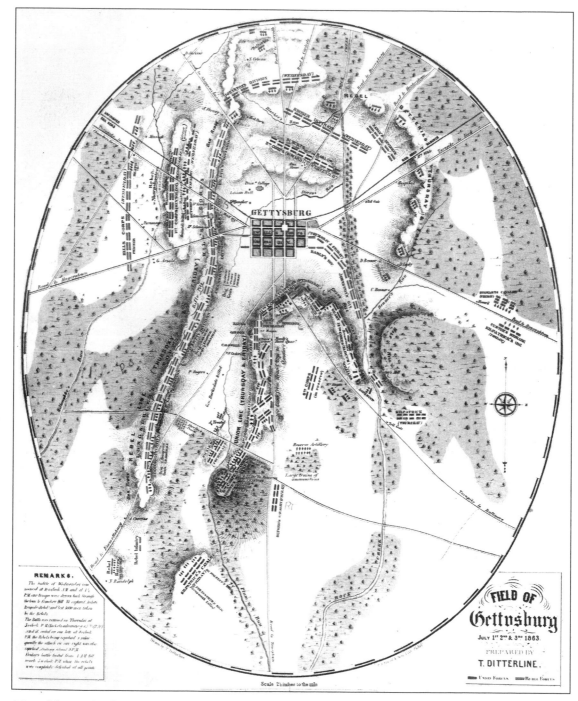

Map of the Battle of Gettysburg.

Union soldiers killed at Gettysburg.

push back their opponents, the Northern horsemen surprised them with their skill; for the first time since the war began, Federal cavalry were able to almost match their Southern counterparts on the battlefield.

During the next two weeks, the Northern army regrouped, waiting while Abraham Lincoln prepared to replace its disliked and largely ineffective commander, Joseph Hooker. All the while, the 100,000-man Army of the Potomac tracked Confederate troop movement and guarded the Union capital of Washington, D.C. In order for Lee to attain the Confederate objective—to win a military victory over a superior enemy—it was essential for him to choose the most propitious conditions under which to fight.

Lee entrusted cavalry commander Major General Jeb Stuart to discern the exact location, size, and intent of the Union army. Stuart, however, miserably failed his commander. Instead of performing quick forays and returning to camp, he embarked on a raid similar to the one that gained him much fame during the Peninsula campaign. In this case, however, his largely unsuccessful efforts took him out of Lee's range as he rode around the Union's seemingly endless rear.

For more than two crucial weeks, Lee had no idea of the Union army's location or strength; he did not learn that his enemy had crossed the Potomac heading northwest until June 28. As it marched toward the Pennsylvania city of Harrisburg, northeast of Gettysburg, the Army of the Potomac moved with a new enthusiasm sparked by its new commander, the well-respected Major General George Meade.

In the meantime, Lee, whose hopes of surprising the enemy had been dashed, ordered his troops to stop their advance and converge west of Gettysburg until word from Stuart arrived. On July 1, a group of Confederates under Major General Henry Heth, innocently hoping to find a supply of new shoes in town, headed into Gettysburg. Encamped on a hill to the southwest of town, the Union cavalry commander, Brigadier General John Buford spotted the enemy troops, deployed his men, and called for reinforcements. After the Confederate soldiers reported the Union troop movements back to camp, a Confederate attack upon the newly formed Union cavalry line was ordered, thus beginning the Battle of Gettysburg.

The Union force was ready with new troops from the 1st Corps, led by Major General John F. Reynolds. Heth's division then stormed into Reynolds' line on McPherson's Ridge, killing Reynolds and devastating one of his best-fighting units, the Iron Brigade of the West. The Confederates seized the ridge, pushing the Federals back to Seminary Ridge. In the meantime, the battle had attracted troops from both sides in great numbers. The Union

troops were converging from the south and east, while the Confederates came from the north and west.

On this first day, the Confederates outnumbered the Federals three to two, another rare occurrence. In the afternoon, the Confederates used their greater numbers to good advantage, driving Northern troops led by Major General Winfield Scott Hancock through the town of Gettysburg to Cemetery Ridge, just south of town. An immediate and vigorous Confederate attack on the hills might have succeeded, but General Richard Ewell, under orders from Lee to attack "if possible," decided not to attempt such a risky venture in the waning hours of daylight.

During the night, both Union and Confederate troops regrouped. The Union position on the morning of July 2 resembled a huge fishhook, the shank of it located at Cemetery Ridge, a long low ridge running north-south and dominated at each end by hills; the bent part of the hook curved around the ridge and ended with its barb on Cemetery Hill and Culp's Hill to the east. The high hills (Little Round Top and Round Top) to the south were unoccupied.

The Confederates were divided on how to attack the Union position. Lieutenant General James Longstreet argued for a flanking movement beyond the Union left which might force the Union to attack, while Lee pushed for a more offensive approach. One aim was to secure one or both of the high hills upon which the Confederates could mount artillery. Early in the afternoon, Union Major General Daniel E. Sickles, on his own initiative, moved his corps about one mile forward of the main line of defense to occupy a peach orchard and wheat field, thus weakening the Union left just as the Confederates planned to attack. Longstreet, however, delayed deployment of troops, then delivered a half-hearted thrust at the hills at about 4 p.m. In the meantime, Meade had become aware of the Confederate plans for the Round Tops and diverted troops to reinforce Sickles.

In the early evening hours, both sides fought raging battles in the peach orchard, wheat field, and a mass of boulders that earned the nickname "Devil's Den" after the carnage that took place there that day. Meade's quick maneuvers saved Little Round Top and secured the Union position. Later, Confederate troops made valiant efforts to take Cemetery Hill and Culp's Hill, but only made slight headway before being overwhelmed by the Union.

Exhausted and severely depleted, both armies faced another day of heavy fighting on July 3. It began at daylight on the north end of the line, when Union General Henry W. Slocum's troops managed to retake its positions near Culp's Hill. As the armies prepared for the major coordinated assault that was sure to come, Longstreet again urged a flanking maneuver to force the Union to assume the offensive. Lee vetoed him once again, feeling he had no choice but to either admit defeat or try one more assault.

His strikes at the Union flanks having failed, Lee issued orders for an attack directed at the center of the Union line at Culp's Hill. Spearheaded by Major General George E.

Pickett's fresh division, the offensive would involve 15,000 Confederate men. At the same time, Lee ordered the newly arrived Jeb Stuart to attack the Union rear from the east with his cavalry.

The last battle of the engagement began at 1:00 p.m. with a tremendous Artillery duel, which continued until both armies were almost out of ammunition. Pickett's Charge, an ill-fated and desperate attempt by the Confederates to storm Cemetery Ridge, began at about 3:30 p.m. A full contingent of soldiers marched across an open field while Union artillery fire mowed them down. A few men managed to reach the Union position and capture a short stretch of the line, but finally could not hold it. Jeb Stuart's three-hour assault on the Confederate rear flank was equally devastating to the Confederate position. At the end of the day, Lee admitted defeat to his battered men, saying to them, "It's all my fault. My fault."

The losses at Gettysburg were horrifying, even in a war known for its carnage. Of the 85,000 Union forces at Gettysburg, more than 23,000 were killed, wounded, captured or missing; the Confederates lost 20,000 of their 70,000 troops. On the evening of July 4, just as word reached Richmond that the Confederates at Vicksburg had capitulated, Robert E. Lee began his retreat to Virginia. Had the Union army pursued and attacked, the war may have ended then and there. Exhausted and aware of the South's tenacity, Meade decided to let Lee fall back. The war would rage on for nearly two more years.

★ ★ ★

Ruins of the bridge at Harpers Ferry, 1862.

Harpers Ferry, Capture of

SEPTEMBER 15, 1862

A crucial element in General Robert E. Lee's strategy to invade the North during his Antietam campaign concerned the capture of the federal garrison of 11,000 men in Harpers Ferry. While Lee took one division up to Hagarstown, Pennsylvania, and sent another division to guard Boonseboro Gap with Daniel H. Hill, he ordered Thomas "Stonewall" Jackson to capture the garrison with nearly half of Lee's 36,000-man army. Jackson then divided his own forces into three groups, each approaching from a differ-

ent direction to effectively seal the town and garrison. Built on low ground surrounded by hills now swarming with Confederates, the Union fort, under the command of Colonel Dixon S. Miles, was in an untenable position, making surrender or utter carnage inevitable.

Remarkably, however, a contingent of 1,300 cavalry, led by Colonel Benjamin F. Davis, managed to fight their way out of the garrison and fled to Union lines. On the way, they captured a Confederate ammunition train of 97 wagons and its escort of 600 men without losing a single man themselves. The rest of the garrison troops, however, were forced to surrender after the first round of artillery fire from Jackson's forces. Jackson's victory netted the Confederates invaluable supplies, including 13,000 small arms and 73 cannon. After securing the garrison, Jackson sped with his troops to join the less-than-successful Confederate offensive at Antietam.

Kennesaw Mountain, Battle of
JUNE 27, 1864

The battle at Kennesaw Mountain, Georgia, will long be remembered as one of the bloodiest segments of the Atlanta Campaign between William T. Sherman and Joseph E. Johnston. The Union Armies of the Tennessee and the Cumberland, aided by the Army of the Ohio, faced Johnston's Army of Tennessee near Marietta, Georgia; several days of skirmishing and maneuvering in relentlessly rainy weather finally erupted in conflict as the Federals attacked the well entrenched positions of the Confederates. Charging uphill, the Union forces were able to do little more than gain small footholds. The main line was so strong as to be nearly impregnable, for Johnston had taken excellent advantage of the rock-strewn landscape.

Sherman has been often criticized, then and now, for making three concentrated assaults on Johnston's front to heavy losses. The end result was an expensive embarrassment for Sherman and a moral victory as well as a military one for Johnston; however, the Confederate commander would increasingly from this point adopt a tactic of withdrawing

and refusing unless pushed to actively engage the enemy. He would earn for himself first the nickname of "Retreating Joe," and then the disapproval of his president, leading to his being relieved of command in favor of the more aggressive John Bell Hood. Sherman would continue to pick at and maneuver around the Confederate lines until his objective, Atlanta, was reached in September 1864.

Manassas (First), Campaign and Battle of
JULY 16–21, 1861

The first battle of the Civil War was fought at Manassas Junction, Virginia, near a creek called Bull Run. Confederate forces at Manassas were led by General Pierre T. Beauregard, while General Irvin McDowell led the Federal army. At First Manassas, also known as First Bull Run, the South successfully stopped the Union's advance toward Richmond, the Confederate capital.

Manassas (Second), Campaign and Battle of
AUGUST 26–SEPTEMBER 1, 1862

Second Manassas, also known as Second Bull Run, was fought over the same territory as First Manassas. Confederate troops under the

Six marines with fixed bayonets.

leadership of Major Generals Robert E. Lee and James Longstreet clashed with the Union forces of Major Generals George McClellan and John Pope. Despite being outnumbered, the South won this battle, and the North retreated back to Washington, D.C.

Marine Corps, Confederate

On March 16, 1861, the Confederate Congress established the Confederate States Marine Corps (CSMC). Commanded largely by former United States Marine officers, the CSMC played a relatively small role in the Civil War. Its highest level of enrollment was approximately 540 enlisted men and officers. As in most branches of the armed services, the CSMC suffered from desertions and a lack of new recruits as the war continued; the fact that the pay of enlisted marines was $3 less per month than that of equivalent army grades did not help matters. Confederate marines served mainly as guard detachments for naval stations at Confederate ports and as personnel at naval shore batteries along the Southern coast. The largest engagement involving Confederate marines was at the battle of the *Monitor* vs. the *Merrimack* (CSS *Virginia*) at Hampton Roads, Virginia, from March 8 to 9, 1862.

Marines, United States

Like their Confederate counterparts, United States Marines played a limited role in the Civil War. A lack of cooperation between the navy and the army accounted for their virtual invisibility. A branch of the Department of the Navy, its commanders, Marine Commandant John C. Harris (1861–1864) and his successor Major Jacob Zeilin, generally steered clear of all army operations. In addition, at the start of the war, the corps suffered from a shortage of personnel, especially after most of its officers resigned to join the Confederacy. By 1864, however, the corps operated at full-strength; with 5,000 enlisted marines serving as ship guards and manning naval batteries. Most of the shore operations in which the U.S. Marines participated were unsuccessful, including First Bull Run and Fort Fisher. Altogether, approximately 150 Union marines were killed in action during the Civil War.

Mobile Bay, Battle of
AUGUST 5, 1864

This naval engagement determined the fate of the Confederacy's last major open Gulf port east of Texas. While the Union blockade was in place elsewhere, Alabama's Mobile Bay became a center for the receipt of critically needed provisions smuggled into the South from Europe. U.S. Rear Admiral David G.

Farragut wanted to try taking the port after he captured New Orleans in April 1862, but he was not able to begin his preparations until January 1864.

After more than half a year of planning, Farragut's fleet of 14 wooden ships and four ironclads began its attack shortly after dawn on August 5, entering the bay's heavily mined main channel at 6 a.m., with the monitors in front. The Confederates started firing as the Union boats approached the bay's main defense, Fort Morgan. Leading a flotilla of three small, wooden gunboats and the CSS *Tennessee*—the South's largest ironclad—Confederate Admiral Franklin Buchanan commanded the defensive naval forces against an attack for which he had prepared for two years.

Farragut had himself lashed to the mast of his flagship, the *Hartford*, so he could better direct his forces, and watched as his lead ironclad, the *Tecumseh*, struck a mine. Blown out of the water, the ship sank in minutes with most of its crew. The Federal fleet halted in alarm as the firing continued from Fort Morgan, until Farragut's famous command, "Damn the torpedoes! Full speed ahead." Moving the *Hartford* in front, the Union admiral led his fleet through the minefield with no additional sinkings and past the fort into the bay.

The *Tennessee*, with Buchanan aboard, attempted to ram the Union ships, then traded fire with the vessels before taking refuge at Fort Morgan. While the Union crews began taking the opportunity to have some breakfast, Buchanan pulled the *Tennessee* out from the fort for another attack. The Confederate ironclad, imposing but unwieldy, was quickly surrounded by Federal boats and fired on and rammed repeatedly. Soon adrift and helpless, with commander Buchanan himself seriously wounded, the *Tennessee* surrendered at approximately 10 a.m., and the battle was over.

Union forces, which totaled nearly 3,000, suffered 319 casualties; of the 470 Confederates engaged, there were 312 casualties, most taken as prisoner. The Union navy now effectively controlled Mobile Bay for the remainder of the war, although Fort Morgan was not captured until August 23, and the city of Mobile itself, 30 miles to the north, remained in Confederate control until the following April—three days, in fact, after Lee surrendered.

The *Monitor* vs. the Merrimack (CSS *Virginia*)
MARCH 8, 1862

Ushering in a revolution in sea combat, the single, inconclusive March 1862 encounter between the Union and the Confederacy's first ironclads was perhaps the most sensational naval battle of the Civil War.

The *Merrimack* (sometimes spelled without the "k") had been one of the U.S. Navy's finest wood steam frigates before Northern forces scuttled it when they were forced to abandon the Norfolk shipyards one week after the fall of Fort Sumter. Salvaging the wreck in the summer of 1861, Confederate engineers bolted 2- to 4-inch-thick armor plates on the hull and deck,

constructed casemate ports for ten guns, and fitted a cast-iron ram to the prow. Most of the peculiar-looking vessel was submerged, with the exposed portion sloped on a 35-degree angle to increase the chances that enemy shells would simply ricochet off its sides. Slow and unwieldy, too unseaworthy for ocean service yet with too deep a draft for shallow rivers, it was still a fearsome craft that could outmatch any wooden ship that came against it.

Reports of the refashioned *Merrimack,* renamed the CSS *Virginia,* drifted north and compelled the Union navy to hasten its own efforts at building an ironclad. The renowned Swedish-American inventor, John Ericsson, who had been tinkering with armored vessel designs for 20 years, developed a unique new ship for the North, protected by four and one half inches of iron plating, with two guns mounted on an innovative revolving turret. Smaller, swifter, and more maneuverable than the *Merrimack,* the *Monitor,* also mostly submerged, was an even odder-looking vessel, described as resembling a "cheesebox on a raft."

Construction was completed in a remarkable 101 days, beating the South's ironclad to the launching slip, and on March 4, 1862, the *Monitor* was towed out of Brooklyn, New York, to join the Federal blockading squadrons off the Carolina coast.

The CSS *Virginia* (though it often remains better known by its former name), was launched at Norfolk Shipyard on March 5. Its crew thinking they were on a trial run, the Confederate ship headed right for battle at Hampton Roads, Virginia, a channel off Newport News at the entrance of the Chesapeake Bay that was a major Union blockading base.

At about 1 p.m. on March 8, the *Virginia* confronted a fleet of five wooden Federal ships. Enemy broadsides bounced off the ironclad as it rammed and sank the *Cumberland*, the Union's mightiest frigate, ran aground and burned the 50-gun *Congress*, and incapacitated the huge flagship *Minnesota* before withdrawing for the night. The Union navy would not suffer such great losses again until the World War II attack on Pearl Harbor. Though its ram had broken off in the fighting and its captain, Franklin Buchanan, had been wounded, the *Virginia* was little damaged, poised to destroy the rest of the Hampton Roads fleet and then to go on and threaten the entire Union blockade.

The *Monitor*'s hasty arrival in the channel at 1 a.m. on March 9 did not initially calm the mounting panic in Washington, D.C. Nearly sinking on its voyage south, the Union vessel seemed barely able to float, let alone fight. But in battle, the *Monitor* proved an equal match to the *Virginia*. Only 100 yards apart, the two ironclads began a furious four-hour duel at 9 a.m. that morning, pounding out artillery fire that scarcely made a dent and colliding several times, both accidentally and in unsuccessful attempts to ram each other. Neither ship could gain the advantage, and when the *Monitor* pulled back after its captain, John L. Worden, was temporarily blinded by a shell blast, the *Virginia*, beginning to leak and have engine problems, withdrew.

The first battle in history between iron-

The USS Monitor *and the CSS* Merrimack *(renamed the CSS* Virginia*) at war.*

clads ended in a draw, though the Union blockade at Hampton Roads held and the North's fears of losing its naval superiority were allayed. Still, the Confederacy proved it could mount a formidable challenge to the Union fleet, as both sides acknowledged the obvious superiority of armored ships and hurried to build more.

The *Monitor* and the *Virginia*, however, never confronted each other again—neither, in fact, remained afloat for long. On May 11, little more than two months after the *Virginia* was launched, the Confederates blew up their pioneer ironclad in Norfolk harbor to prevent its seizure by Union forces that had captured the port. And on December 31, the *Monitor* sank in a storm off the coast of Cape Hatteras, North Carolina.

Morgan's Raids
OCTOBER 1862–JULY 1863

Confederate Brigadier General John Hunt Morgan's three spectacular cavalry raids in Kentucky and Tennessee so disrupted the Union army in the west that President Abraham Lincoln himself sent an urgent missive to commander Henry W. Halleck: "They are having a stampede in Kentucky. Please look to it."

John Hunt Morgan—the epitome of a cavalry commander sitting straight, tall, and fearless in the saddle—had served in the Mexican War but otherwise had no professional military training. He began his Civil

War service as captain, incorporating the Lexington Rifles, a local militia he had organized in 1857, into the Confederate effort when the war began. By the end of 1862, he had been made a brigadier general in command of the 2nd Kentucky Cavalry and was serving under Major General Joseph Wheeler in the western theater.

Morgan's first raid undermined Union Major General Don Carlos Buell's attempts to capture Chattanooga, Tennessee. From July 4 to August 1, 1862, he and his men covered more than 1,000 miles, captured more than 1,200 prisoners, and destroyed several Union supply depots along the way. Morgan himself lost just 100 men.

Three months later, after serving under General Braxton Bragg during his Kentucky campaign, the clever horseman and his unit joined Lieutenant General Kirby Smith as he attempted to retreat from Kentucky while under fire from pursuing Union troops. With 1,800 men, he circled eastward, captured Lexington, Kentucky, and destroyed Union transportation and communication lines before returning to Tennessee at the beginning of November.

Morgan's third raid, also known as his "Christmas Raid," was designed to help Bragg counter Union Major General William S. Rosecrans' advance through Tennessee. After organizing a division of two brigades totalling about 4,000 men, Morgan headed north from Alexandria, Tennessee, on December 21, 1862, to raid Rosecrans' lines of communication and supply.

Riding through Glasgow and Bardstown, he reached the Louisville & Nashville Railroad and followed it to Rolling Fork, near Elizabethtown, capturing the town and severing Rosecrans' lines.

By this time, the Union army had tracked the cavalrymen and were preparing to attack them as they headed back to Confederate lines. Morgan, realizing the danger, made his escape during the night with minimal loss of life, returning to camp on January 2, 1863. In just over a week, he and his men managed to destroy more than two million dollars worth of Union property and capture about 1,900 troops.

Morgan's final raid took place during July 1863. While his commander, Braxton Bragg, had directed him merely to slow Rosecrans' advance on Chattanooga, Morgan instead invaded Ohio. He hoped that a show of Confederate strength would raise support for the Southern cause among Yankees who were both tired of the war and sympathetic in some manner to the South. Although he did inflict damage on the Union supply lines, this raid appeared to more like a reckless adventure than a well-planned offensive. On July 2, Morgan managed to elude more than 10,000 Union troops and took about 2,500 men across the Cumberland River. Wreaking his usual havoc on his way north, he joined in several skirmishes with Federals while completing the longest continuous march of the war, covering 90 miles in just 35 hours.

On the afternoon of July 13, he arrived in Harrison, Ohio, with a reduced force of 2,000 and with the Union already planning his capture. Indeed, his men had already captured 6,000 men, mobilized thousands of Union troops, destroyed 25 bridges, and demolished scores of railroads. By July 18, however, Morgan began to encounter serious enemy action; the next day, he was badly beaten by forces under Union Brigadier General Edward H. Hobson at Buffington Island. Supported by militia and gunboats, the Union troops managed to devastate Morgan's crew, killing about 120 and capturing another 700.

Morgan himself managed to escape with about 300 men and made a desperate effort to reach Pennsylvania. Hobson pursued relentlessly, finally capturing the wily horseman on July 26, at New Lisbon. Morgan and his raiders were then imprisoned in the Ohio State Penitentiary. Remarkably, Morgan was able to escape, although he was killed just about a month later during a cavalry encounter at Greeneville, Tennessee, on September 3, 1864.

Murfreesboro, Battle of

DECEMBER 31, 1862–
JANUARY 2, 1863

The close of the war's first full year brought action at last on the Tennessee front between Confederate defender Braxton Bragg and his Union opponent William S. Rosecrans. After several days of impending attack, both generals curiously enough came to nearly exact conclusions: it was the last day of the year, they must make some sort of demonstration, and it would be to fling the left extreme of their line against the right flank of the enemy. Bragg, however, put his plan into motion while Rosecrans was still trying to feel his way; just after dawn William Hardee sent his corps smashing into the Union right. This set what would be the Federal standard for the day, as Rosecrans' forces remained essentially on the defensive throughout the fighting.

As each Confederate move was made, a mirror maneuver was enacted on the Union side to attempt to counter it; the Federals fell back to the difficult position of trying to hold the turnpike which ran between Murfreesboro and Nashville, with Stone's River at their back—never a good tactical position in which to find oneself, but worse in the dead of winter with the water high and cold. Constantly under attack from the cavalry under General Joseph Wheeler, and knowing he was in a daunting position, Rosecrans ordered the assault abandoned and concentrated his line on the turnpike. The fighting continued without conclusion until well into the afternoon; the Federals held on stubbornly, inflicting heavy casualties on the Confederates.

By the end of the day, the two armies settled in for a long, cold night, each expecting to continue in the morning. In one of the more poignant incidents of the war, a military band on one side began to play "Home, Sweet Home." As the notes sounded across the cold ground that had been a killing field in the daylight, a band on the opposing side joined in to play along in the darkness. In the silence that followed the tune, the two armies caught what little sleep they could almost within sight of one another on the field of battle.

The Confederates used the darkness to entrench; the Federal commanders met in an attempt to design a new strategy. After much discussion, it was decided they would remain and fight it out. Curiously enough, however, as the new day and new year dawned, almost nothing of a military nature occurred; there were occasional sporadic outbreaks of firing, and once or twice a brief artillery duel, but neither army came forward on the muddy ground to offer battle.

It was not until the early morning hours of January 2, 1863, that anything substantive happened—and that turned out to be very gallant, very bloody, and tactically pointless. Confederate John C. Breckinridge led his men to take a hill to the northeast of Stone's River, which they did with accompanying high casualties, only to be attacked in force and pushed back by superior strength bolstered by a shattering artillery barrage. The two armies did nothing more for the rest of the day, but sat back to contemplate their heavy losses: between wounded, killed or missing, the Federal forces had been depleted by almost 13,000 out of over 40,000; the Confederates suffered nearly 12,000 out of 35,000 men lost or no longer able to fight.

There was a brief attack the following day, January 3, as the Federals demonstrated against Bragg's lines near the river, but very little came of it, and there was no return to the general conflict. The Federals were astounded but gratified when, for no reason they could see, Bragg withdrew his forces from Murfreesboro along the Manchester Turnpike for the next day or so. Rosecrans moved his men into the town on January 5, 1863, and was wired by Abraham Lincoln that he had the admiration and congratulations of his country for the victory. Two weeks later, on January 21, Braxton Bragg discovered what his country thought of him for his curious retreat: President Jefferson Davis sent General Joseph E. Johnston to investigate the Army of Tennessee's commander, looking into reasons he had for abandoning Murfreesboro, and to see if there was any substance to criticisms of Bragg that had reached Richmond. Bragg would not be relieved of command, but Davis' confidence in him was seriously impaired for a long time to come.

Nashville, Battle of

DECEMBER 15–16, 1864

The Confederate Army of Tennessee under John Bell Hood was crushed after a two day onslaught by George Henry Thomas' Union troops outside Nashville in December 1864, a decisive clash that ended the major fighting in the Civil War's western theater.

Fresh from the catastrophic November 30 defeat at Franklin, 75 miles south of the state capital, Hood refused to abandon his quixotic invasion of Tennessee, still irrationally hoping his army could retake the state, collect reinforcements, and mount new assaults on Union forces in Virginia and the Ohio Valley. Also thinking that a retreat would invite large-scale desertion, the undaunted Confederate commander ordered his demoralized troops—one quarter of whom were marching barefoot—forward toward Nashville. There, they faced a Union force twice as large as their own—Thomas' 30,000 troops, sent earlier by William T. Sherman to ward off the Confederate advance, joined by John Schofield's equally large army that had just come up from Franklin.

Occupying the Tennessee capital since early 1862, the Union military had already turned the city into a near-impenetrable fortress. By the time Hood's army arrived in the hills a few miles south on December 2, there was little the Confederates could do either to dislodge or pass the enemy. With far too few troops for an effective siege or a direct assault, and unable to advance around the city without exposing their rear and flank, the Southerners dug in and formed a wide defensive line, hoping for reinforcements and waiting for Thomas' attack.

Recognizing his adversary's dire position, the methodical Union commander took his time preparing his army's offensive. Back in Virginia, Ulysses S. Grant was livid at the delay. Overestimating Hood and underestimating Thomas, the Union general-in-chief feared that the Army of Tennessee was poised to prolong the nearly concluded war by invading Northern territory and wired several urgent messages to Nashville ordering an immediate attack. Thomas ignored the directives as he waited for a heavy sleet storm to pass, while Grant headed to Tennessee to relieve the general and take charge of the operation himself.

Before he arrived, Thomas struck at last. On the morning of December 15, three Union corps began hammering the Confederate left while an ancillary infantry and cavalry attack

The 1st Tennessee Colored Battery on its way to Nashville, November 23, 1864.

kept Southern troops busy at the other end of the line. Barely holding on until sundown, Hood's army finally fell back two miles that night to a new defensive position extending between two hills.

Thomas did not know whether the Confederates had retreated altogether in the dark and waited until the following afternoon to mount a renewed assault. Hood's troops were able to repel a charge on Overton Hill to their right, but by 4 p.m. his entire left flank was virtually surrounded by Union infantry, cavalry, and artillery. Smashing suddenly through the line with astonishing force as a hard rain fell, the Northerners utterly routed the Confederate army. Nearly an entire divi-

sion—cannon and all—was captured as hundreds of Southern troops surrendered, while others abandoned their weapons and supplies to flee more quickly.

Followed closely by Union horsemen, the splintered remnants of the Army of Tennessee continued retreating for the next two weeks all the way to Mississippi, covered in the rear by Nathan Bedford Forrest's fighting cavalry. For such a conclusive battle, the casualties were surprisingly light—fewer than 400 Federals killed and about 1,500 Confederates killed or wounded. But with its twin defeats at Franklin and Nashville and its subsequent headlong retreat, John Bell Hood's army was demolished.

In January 1865, the general resigned a command that had all but ceased to exist, while most of his surviving troops were sent back into combat in the East to stem Sherman's unstoppable advance through the Carolinas.

Navy

Both the Federal and Confederate navies played crucial roles in the Civil War; the Union blockade and naval operations in the western theater were at least as important to the Northern victory as its successful land war. Moreover, the technical and strategic advances made by both sides during the period effectively ushered in the era of modern warfare at sea.

When the Civil War began, neither the Union nor the Confederacy had strong naval capabilities. The Union had just 90 ships, half of which were out of commission. Its 1,500 officers and 75,000 enlisted men were scattered around the globe; more than 10 percent of its officers would resign to join the Confederacy. Another Union loss to the Confederacy near the beginning of the war was the Norfolk Navy Yard on April 20–21, 1861. However, with its vast industrial and financial resources, the Union quickly established a naval force powerful enough to devastate the South.

Gunboat USS Mendota.

At the beginning of the war, the Confederate navy consisted of just 10 ships and 15 guns, and it would struggle throughout the war to maintain its ranks at full strength. At the time of the Civil War, the world's navies were just making the transition from sail to steam and from wooden ships to ironclads. To compensate for its dearth of resources, the Confederate navy attempted to appropriate some of these new technologies. The South was the first to build an ironclad, to experiment with submarine technology, and to use torpedoes during battle (at Yorktown, Virginia, May 1862).

Without question, the major naval operation of the war, for both sides, was the Northern blockade of Southern ports. Under orders from U.S. Navy Secretary Gideon Welles, the Union concentrated its force along the Southern coast in order to strangle the Confederate government economically. David Farragut's capture of New Orleans on April 25, 1862, solidified Union control of the seas. In turn, most of the South's scant naval resources were devoted to efforts at circumventing the blockade; in fact, Confederate Secretary of the Navy Stephen Mallory was criticized for spending too much time and money on building blockade runners and in conducting raids on Northern shipping, neither of which did much damage to the blockade in the end. In fact, the North's foreign trade actually increased between 1861 and 1865, while the South's barely survived.

Second in importance only to the blockade were U.S. naval operations on the western rivers. With their potent firepower, Union gunboats helped to capture Fort Henry, Fort Donelson, and Vicksburg, thereby providing secure arteries for moving Union men and matériel across an otherwise impenetrable landscape of lowland mire.

The number of successful combined navy-army operations was limited, however, largely due to lack of a proper chain of command and cooperation between the two branches of the service. In addition, naval commanders, convinced of the ironclads' invincibility, often underestimated the need for the army's help to subdue the enemy. By the end of the war, due to its vast technical and industrial advances, the U.S. Navy had become one of the most powerful forces in the world, with more than 600 ships and 50,000 men.

New Orleans, Battle of
APRIL 25, 1862

David Farragut's impressive April 1862 naval victory placed the Confederacy's largest city and most vital port in the hands of the Union. A hundred miles above the mouth of the Mississippi, New Orleans was the gateway to the great river and to the entire deep South, and its capture could almost divide the Confederacy in two. Military actions elsewhere left the city itself lightly defended, dependent on the protection of Forts Jackson and St. Philip, which guarded the river approach 75 miles downstream. But the garrisons were heavily fortified, and a barricade of hulks in the water stalled vessels right in front of their heavy guns.

Battle of New Orleans.

With Union naval commander David Porter arguing that sustained mortar fire from boats on the river would disable the forts and allow a fleet of ships to pass all the way to New Orleans, preparations were begun for the attempt in early 1862. Army General Benjamin Butler captured Ship Island near the mouth of the Mississippi, where David Farragut, squadron captain and Porter's adopted brother, gathered 24 wooden sloops and gunboats, along with Porter's 19 mortar schooners. After delays to make the vessels light enough to pass over the many sand bars, Farragut's fleet started ascending the river in April, supported by 15,000 troops under Butler for possible land battle.

On April 18, Porter commenced a six-day barrage of cannon fire on the two forts, an incessant bombardment of over 3,000 shells a day that did more to rattle Union crews with the constant pounding than to weaken the Confederate defenses. Perhaps distracted by the shelling, however, the Southerners did not seem to notice when two Federal gunboats approached the river barricade on the night of April 20 and cleared a small passageway through. With Porter's bombardment making little impact, Farragut ordered his fleet to proceed anyway. Hidden by the dark, the boats started their audacious run at 2 a.m. on April 24.

Cannon fire from the forts, answered by Union shelling from the river, quickly lit up the sky in a dazzling nighttime fireworks display. Their two nearby ironclads not yet fully operational, the Confederates launched a small squadron of wooden ships to ram the Federal boats and sent rafts set ablaze to impede the advance. Farragut's flagship, the *Hartford,* caught fire and ran aground, but was afloat again shortly as the Union fleet proceeded to sink or disable the enemy vessels. After an hour and a half of pounding battle, all but four of Farragut's boats managed to pass the Confederate forts, despite some heavy damage and nearly 170 men killed or injured.

On April 25, Farragut steamed into New Orleans, defended now only by angry pistol-bearing citizens, and captured the city without further combat, though the mayor refused to formally surrender. Butler's troops arrived on April 29, beginning their harsh occupation, while the day before, Forts Jackson and St. Philip, whose disheartened soldiers had begun to mutiny, surrendered, too.

It was a disastrous defeat for the South. Although the Union did not yet control the entire Mississippi, the entrance to the water-

way that bisected the Confederacy and served as its lifeline would remain cut off for the rest of the war.

Peninsula Campaign
MARCH–AUGUST 1862

The direct approach to the Confederate capital having failed at First Bull Run, commander-in-chief of the Federal armies, George B. McClellan, planned to attack Richmond, Virginia, by-passing what he believed was an enormous Confederate force led by Major General Joseph E. Johnston at Manassas Junction. Transporting his men by ship down the Chesapeake Bay to the mouth of the Rappahannock, he would then lead them on foot across the peninsula to Richmond before Johnston could stop him. Although taking this course would leave Washington, D.C., exposed to the Rebel army, Lincoln—desperate for any action—agreed to the plan.

On March 17, McClellan began his advance. About 400 vessels carried more than 100,000 men from the Washington area to Fortress Monroe at the tip of the Virginia peninsula. Once ashore, however, poor weather, impassable roads, and flooding considerably slowed his march. On April 5, the Union advance reached Yorktown, where about 11,000 Confederates, led by the wily John Bankhead Magruder, waited in a solid defensive position.

Although vastly outnumbered by McClellan, Magruder used tricks—including march-

Federal encampment at Cumberland Landing, Virginia, during the Peninsula Campaign.

ing one battalion in and out of a clearing several times—to convince McClellan that his force was enormous. Instead of attacking and annihilating his enemy, McClellan cabled Washington to send reinforcements. "It seems clear that I shall have the whole force of the enemy on my hands," he wrote, and informed Lincoln that he was settling in for a siege on Yorktown.

Lincoln begged the commander to push ahead, but McClellan refused. For more than a month, he did little more than wait, allowing Johnston to bring most of his army onto the peninsula to oppose his advance. Nevertheless, McClellan's troops could still easily overwhelm Johnston's 60,000 men.

On May 3, with 100 Federal guns in place, McClellan was at last prepared to attack. That night, the Confederates surprised the Union army by launching a massive artillery attack. The surprise turned to shock in the morning when they realized that the Confederates had abandoned Yorktown during the barrage, retreating to a better defensive position to the south at Williamsburg. McClellan ordered his men to pursue and attack the Confederate line.

A brutal day of fighting ensued, with the Confederates losing about 1,700 men and the Union about 2,200, until the Rebels were forced to resume their withdrawal up the peninsula. By doing so, the Confederates essentially surrendered most of eastern Virginia, including Norfolk Naval Yard. The Confederate navy was forced to destroy its ironclad, the CSS *Virginia* (*Merrimack*), housed at the yard, to keep the Union from obtaining it.

By the end of May, the two armies opposed each other just outside of Richmond. McClellan again requested reinforcements; specifically he wanted Irvin McDowell and his 40,000-man army to join him. McDowell, however, was occupied with the maneuvering of Stonewall Jackson in the Shenandoah Valley. On May 31, nature struck a blow against McClellan by flooding the Chickahominy River, thus isolating two Union corps near the villages of Fair Oaks and Seven Pines. Johnston immediately took advantage of the situation, ordering corps commanders James Longstreet and William Whitings to make a strong attack. In what one historian called "A Battle of Strange Errors," a series of miscommunications and mistakes on the part of the Confederates turned what might have been a victory into a draw. The day-long battle was a bitter one, however, killing or wounding more than 11,000 men—about 5,000 Federals and 6,000 Confederates.

The battle had two significant results. First, the fierce fighting frightened an already overcautious McClellan, who wrote home that he was "tired of the sickening sight of the battlefield with its mangled corpses and poor wounded." Second, the Confederate failure to fully exploit the situation caused President Jefferson Davis to replace Johnston with a more aggressive leader, Robert E. Lee.

Although McClellan continued to advance slowly during the next few weeks, his Peninsula campaign effectively ended when Lee assumed command. Lee did not plan to simply defend the Confederate capital, but instead devised his own offensive strategy known as the Seven Days Campaign, which pushed McClellan all the way back to Harrison's Landing at the edge of the Potomac.

Perryville, Battle of
OCTOBER 8, 1862

This battle, Kentucky's only major conflict in the war, ranks as one of the stranger fights engaged in by Civil War soldiers. Fought essentially by accident, the battle was precipitated by a Confederate chance encounter with Union reconnaissance troops in search of water on a hot, terribly dry day. The commander of the Union forces at Perryville, the dapper General Don Carlos Buell, had been thrown from his horse the morning of the battle, and so had remained at headquarters taking a leisurely luncheon with General Gilbert, one of his subordinates. Owing to an atmospheric phenomenon concerning the terrain and the direction of the wind, the noise of the battle did not carry back in the direction of headquarters—with the result that Buell was unaware anything was going on and consequently did not field the majority of his troops until after four o'clock in the afternoon. His opponent, Confederate General Braxton Bragg, did not fare significantly better; portions of his army were not present on the field either, still being in the vicinity of nearby Frankfort.

Bragg's second-in-command, Episcopal Bishop and Confederate General Leonidas K. Polk, very nearly got himself captured by the troops of the 87th Indiana Infantry (the Hoosiers), in yet another confused accident in the action of the day. Polk mistook the Hoosiers for Confederates and rode up to them with the command that they cease firing into the ranks of their own army. The 87th's commander, Colonel Shryock, responded with a demand to know who Polk was, since Shryock was certain his fire was directed appropriately. Polk realized he was speaking with the enemy, and made a hasty retreat before his confusion could lead to further embarrassment.

Buell's Federals managed to win the engagement despite the confusion. It was a costly defeat for the Confederates in terms of fighting force, as well as loss of territory; estimates of Bragg's casualties are near a fourth of his available 16,000 men. Buell's losses, on the other hand, taking into account that not all of his men even saw action, run just under one tenth, with a little over 4,000 soldiers killed, missing, or wounded out of 37,000.

In the aftermath of Perryville, both Buell and Bragg would receive censure from their respective presidents, Buell for having failed to destroy the retreating Southerners, and Bragg for failing to hold Kentucky. Buell was relieved of command; Bragg would keep his job a little while longer, owing almost entirely to the patronage of President Jefferson Davis.

Petersburg, Siege of
JUNE 1864–MAY 1865

The climax of the fighting in Virginia was an agonizing 10-month deadlock between deeply entrenched Union and Confederate forces, broken only when the worn-down Southern army was finally unable to withstand a frontal assault.

Nine days after his devastating defeat at Cold Harbor in early June 1864, Ulysses S. Grant furtively began advancing the Army of the Potomac, leaving Robert E. Lee baffled about where the Federals were heading. Grant's target was Petersburg, the vital rail and communications center 20 miles south of Richmond through which most of the Confederate capital's supply lines ran. By capturing Petersburg, the Union commander recognized, he would ensure the capitulation of Richmond.

Army engineers, in an extraordinary feat of construction, briskly built a 2,100 foot pontoon bridge for the huge Federal force to cross the James River, and by June 15, William F. Smith's advance guard of over 10,000 was poised to begin the attack on Petersburg. Unaware that Confederate Pierre G. T. Beauregard had fewer than 2,500 men defending the heavily fortified city, the Union general struck far too cautiously, to the disgust of his troops. Smith still managed to make headway, coming close, in fact, to taking the town, but the Confederates held off the Federals until Lee and the Army of Northern Virginia arrived to fill Petersburg's expansive trenches.

His chances for a quick victory spoiled, Grant commenced a daily artillery bombardment of Petersburg and reluctantly settled in for what he knew would be a long siege. Lee was no happier about the situation. With his vastly outnumbered force pinned down in an urgent defense of the South's capital, the Confederate commander lost the mobility that had been his greatest advantage and suspected that it would be "a mere question of time."

Grant himself wasted little time in putting his superior numbers to use. Constructing a formidable labyrinth of trenches, the Federals extended their line in both directions, swinging down from due east of Richmond more than 40 miles around to the southwest of Petersburg. Lee was forced to do the same, dangerously attenuating Confederate defenses.

The South was so desperate for able bodies to line its defenses that it resorted to using old men, boys—and two unwilling members of the Confederate cabinet.

Life in the trenches was brutal for both sides. Numbing boredom was accompanied by the constant threat from sharpshooters and artillery fire. Burrowed in dirt and filth, exposed to the summer heat and the winter cold, the troops suffered even greater losses through disease. But while the Federals were regularly reinforced and kept decently fed and supplied, the Confederates nearly starved, and with thousands deserting or surrendering simply to get food, their numbers diminished further.

Yet, Lee's position was still sufficiently fortified to hold off a Union assault. One audacious attempt to break the Confederate

The 1st Pennsylvania Light Artillery on the front lines at Petersburg.

A captured Confederate encampment at Petersburg.

defense in late July, the "Battle of the Crater," was a fiasco. After a regiment of Pennsylvania coal miners set off a huge explosion in a 500-foot tunnel dug right under the enemy, advancing Union troops were pulverized when they were trapped in the deep hole created by the blast.

The Federals were more successful in tightening the stranglehold on the Southerners. In August, they captured one of Virginia's key lifelines, the Weldon Railroad, after a failed attempt two months earlier. In October, Union forces repulsed a Confederate attempt to retake two vital roads, though later in the month they were unable to seize the Southside Railroad. By late winter 1865, Grant's army had grown to nearly 125,000 with reinforcements, while Lee's had dwindled to under 50,000.

With the besieging Union forces threatening to encircle him, the Confederate commander's one remote chance to survive involved leaving the Petersburg trenches and combining forces with Joseph E. Johnston's army in North Carolina. On March 25, John B. Gordon launched an abrupt attack on the Union line east of the town in an attempt to force the Federals to pull back and to create a breach through which Lee's army could escape south. Capturing Fort Stedman and a half mile of Union trenches, the Confederates seemed close to a breakthrough, only to be forced back after rallying Union troops counterattacked.

To forestall any further such attempts, Grant sent a force miles to the west of the Confederate defenses, trying to stretch Lee's weakened line to the breaking point. On April 1, infantry and cavalry from both sides battled at the Five Forks junction, and George Pickett's Confederate division was routed. When Grant received word of the victory, he ordered the conclusive blow. At 4:30 a.m. the next morning, the Federals launched an overwhelming onslaught along the entire Petersburg front. The Confederates simply could not hold; Union troops smashed through their line at several points.

After sending word to Jefferson Davis that the Confederate capital had to be evacuated, Lee ordered his men to retreat. Petersburg was occupied the evening of April 2, Richmond the following day.

Meanwhile, Lee's army headed west along the Appomattox River—desperately searching for food and for a way to cut south to join Johnston—with Ulysses Grant and the Federals in close pursuit.

Pickett's Charge
JULY 3, 1863

"Whatever my fate, I shall do my duty like a brave man," declared George Pickett just before he led 14,000 Virginians across an open field in one last-gasp effort to win a Confederate victory at Gettysburg.

Pickett's charge on the Union center, July 3, 1863.

After troops led by Richard Ewell had been driven back from Culp's Hill and Jeb Stuart's attack on the Federal rear was foiled, the Confederates' last hope for victory centered on breaking through the Union center at Cemetery Ridge. All afternoon, the Confederates had bombarded the ridge with artillery fire. When an eerie silence descended on the field at about 3:00 p.m., Generals Robert E. Lee and James Longstreet mistakenly assumed they had destroyed the Union batteries and ordered 14,000 Confederate infantry to move forward.

They emerged from the woods on Seminary Ridge and organized themselves into one mile-long line, complete with mounted infantry and colorful battle flags. The only avenue of approach open to the Confederates was across a mile-wide, empty field. With parade-ground precision, the Confederates marched down a small hill. The Union battery had not been destroyed, however; they had merely been saving ammunition to thwart just such an assault.

Within moments after the Confederates started across the field, Union artillery fire began to mow down row after row of the Confederate column. When the thinned-out ranks were within a short distance of the Federal line, their rebel yells could be heard above the thundering of guns as they made their last dash to the front. Although the first line of Federals was driven back upon the earthworks near the artillery, Union fire and a sudden, furious hand-to-hand battle finally stopped the charge. In less than an hour, more than half of the brave men of Pickett's Charge had been killed and nothing had been gained.

The Union claimed victory at Gettysburg and Lee was forced to retreat.

Red River Campaign
MARCH–MAY 1864

Eager to capture the city of Shreveport, Louisiana, and secure East Texas, President Abraham Lincoln authorized an ill-fated expedition up the unpredictable Red River from New Orleans.

Lincoln and his general-in-chief Henry Halleck hoped that a successful thrust into the heartland of Louisiana might convince large numbers of the state's silent Unionists to join the Federal cause. In addition, the Red River area was rich with cotton ready to go to market; at high wartime prices, the incentive for garnering the cotton and selling it to the highest bidder was great.

Although the commander in charge of the expedition, David Dixon Porter, expressed concern about the falling level of the Red River, the plan got underway at the beginning of March. Setting out from New Orleans, Porter took 12 ironclad gunboats, two large wooden steamers, and four smaller steamers. On board were 10,000 men sent by William Tecumseh Sherman and commanded by Brigadier General Andrew J. Smith. Another 15,000 troops, dispatched from the corps of Union General Nathaniel Banks, planned to join them before the contingent reached Shreveport.

Building a dam on the unpredictable Red River.

After achieving initial success at Fort De Russy below Alexandria, Louisiana, the campaign was delayed by weather and bureaucratic maneuvering by Ulysses S. Grant, who wanted to detach Sherman's contingent to proceed with the Atlanta campaign later in April. As Porter headed toward Alexandria, the Red River began to fall and Confederates lining its banks showered the slow-moving flotilla with an endless barrage of small arms and artillery fire.

On land, the army fared no better. Eight thousand Confederate troops led by Major General Richard Taylor forced Banks' men to retreat at Mansfield. In the meantime, Porter, under constant fire, lost a gunboat and a steamer to artillery shells. When he reached Alexandria, the situation grew critical. The water level had plummeted to just three feet; his gunboats needed at least seven feet of water to pass.

Porter faced two equally bleak alternatives: he could destroy his flotilla before the Confederates captured it, or he could watch it, and his men, be devastated by Confederate fire. It was, Porter wrote his mother, "a hard and anxious time" for the admiral and his men. A Wisconsin engineer named Lieutenant Colonel Joseph Bailey, however, saved the day with an ingenious plan. By building a dam across the river, the Union could raise the water level high enough to at least forge a hasty retreat down to the Mississippi.

Approximately 3,000 troops, using nothing but trees, rocks, and bags of dirt, constructed an enormous dam that spanned nearly the whole width of the river.

To finish the job, Porter ordered the sinking of four barges lined up in a row to completely fill the 758-foot expanse. Four of the gunboats managed to pass over the rapids created by the improvised structure before it fell apart; Bailey and his men spent another few days rebuilding before the rest of the squadron could move. Porter's escape to the relative safety of the Mississippi ended the disastrous campaign, gaining nothing for the Union except humiliation.

Salem Church, Battle of
MAY 3–4, 1863

Part of the Battle of Chancellorsville, the fighting around the little edifice known as Salem Church was among the hottest in the larger picture of the campaign.

On the day after Stonewall Jackson's critical wounding, with the main body of the Army of Northern Virginia at the Chancellor house crossroads some ten miles from Fredericksburg, Virginia, preparations were made for an assault that never materialized. The majority of Union General Joseph Hooker's men were in Fredericksburg proper under command of General John Sedgwick, advancing over the old familiar ground of Marye's Heights, scene of the terrible fighting in December 1862, with as little success in the springtime as had been procured the previous winter.

Twice, in action sometimes referred to as the Second Battle of Fredericksburg, Sedgwick's men tried to take the heights; on the third try, after high losses, they finally succeeded in breaking the Confederate line. The Southern defenders, commanded by General Jubal Early, were driven back to the south, leaving the road back to Chancellorsville invitingly open. As Sedgwick accepted the invitation, Robert E. Lee turned his army to meet their advance, using Salem Church as the pivot. All around the small brick church, fighting raged for the remainder of the day until nearly full dark.

That night, the church became a hospital for the wounded and dying of both sides. Badly knocked about and exhausted, the Federals did very little effective movement in the early part of May 4, with the result that Lee was able to bring up the rest of his troops to reinforce Confederate lines around Salem Church. Early moved up from Fredericksburg, and the Federals found themselves assailed from three directions. Unfortunately, the Southern forces had left the back door open, and Sedgwick escaped with his men across the Rappahannock at Banks Ford, crossing the pontoons there under cover of darkness.

Seven Days Campaign
JUNE 25–JULY 1, 1862

Putting an end to the Union's first attempt to capture the Confederate capital of Rich-

Over 15,000 men died in a single day of fighting during the Seven Days Campaign. Here, Federal troops operate Parrott guns.

mond, Robert E. Lee's campaign of deception was a devastating defeat for the Union army. Although the Union technically won almost all seven of the battles fought during the last week of June 1862, the army found itself pushed back all the way to Harrison's Landing, largely because of Union Major General George B. McClellan's fear and indecision.

After the battle of Seven Pines, McClellan divided his army, moving about 80,000 men south of the Chickahominy River. About 20,000 Union troops under Fitz-John Porter remained on the north side of the river to await the arrival of Irwin McDowell's troops on their way from Fredericksburg. As McClellan prepared to move against Richmond, however, Robert E. Lee devised a brilliant plan to move the action away from the capital and take the offensive. His first move was to divide his own army of about 55,000, leaving about 20,000 men with corps commander John Magruder, who would try to detain McClellan, while he himself took about 25,000 men to attack Porter's weak right flank.

The first engagement of the Seven Days Campaign took place on June 25, when a Union reconnaissance division under Joseph

Hooker met Confederate troops at Oak Grove. After a full day of fighting, the Union managed to dislodge the Confederates, but at a loss of more than 625 Federal soldiers. From then on, Lee took the offensive, assisted by his three able corps commanders, Ambrose P. Hill, Daniel H. Hill, and James Longstreet. Also expected to participate was Thomas "Stonewall" Jackson. Exhausted after his successful and brilliant campaign in the Shenandoah Valley, however, Jackson was more a hindrance than a help to Lee.

On June 26, Lee dispatched Hill with five infantry brigades and artillery across the Chickahominy to launch a frontal attack on Porter, who had assumed a defensive position behind Beaver Creek Dam about a mile from a small town called Mechanicsville. In the meantime, Jackson would arrive in time to hit Porter from the rear. Jackson, however, never arrived at the battle site, leaving Hill to attack Porter on his own.

The Confederates fought for more than six hours against a well-prepared Union force; by the end of the day, they had lost nearly 1,500 men while only 360 Union men fell. Under orders from McClellan, Porter then withdrew to another prepared position at Gaines' Mill, which he was ordered to hold at all costs. Hill renewed his attacked there the next morning, only to be stopped by the main Federal line located on a high plateau near Boatswain's Swamp.

Longstreet joined Hill on the Union left in the middle of the afternoon, but was ordered by Lee to delay his attack until Jackson and his men could get in position to hit the opposite flank. Once again, however, Jackson failed to appear when expected, upsetting the battle plan. After a long day of intermittent but heavy skirmishing, the Confederates suddenly launched a full frontal assault, piercing the Federal line.

The day's losses were devastating to both the Union and Confederacy. Out of approximately 34,000 Federals engaged, there were more than 6,800 casualties; about 8,700 out of 57,000 Confederates were lost. Unnerved by Lee's aggression, and believing false reports estimating his enemy's strength at double his own, McClellan ordered a strategic withdrawal.

For the next three days, Lee pursued the retreating Federal army, forcing battles at Savage's Station and White Oak Swamp that did little damage to the Union army but lost him valuable manpower. Nevertheless, his offensive kept the Union army on the run until June 30, when McClellan halted at a strong position on Malvern Hill.

Organizing his defenses throughout the day, McClellan amassed some 250 guns to cover enemy approaches. Although Lee had been warned of the position's impregnability, he decided to attack on the morning of June 1. He first attempted to establish an artillery line of his own, but problems with organization gave the Union the upper hand. Later, as Confederate troops stormed the hill, they were mown down by Union artillery fire. This last day of the campaign was later described by Daniel H. Hill: "It was not war, it was murder." Lee lost more than 5,300 men; McClellan about 3,200.

Despite the fact that McClellan won the battle at Malvern Hill, and even though his corps commanders urged him to hold the position and launch a counterattack, the reticent Union general chose instead to withdraw further. By July 2, he and his troops were entrenched at Harrison's Landing on the James River. Lee would continue his offensive by launching the first eastern invasion of the North by Confederate forces.

Shenandoah Valley Campaign, Jackson's
MAY–JUNE 1862

Swerving, feinting, and racing up and down Virginia's Shenandoah Valley, Thomas J. "Stonewall" Jackson utterly flummoxed three separate Union commands for more than a month in the spring of 1862 in a brilliant series of maneuvers that diverted thousands of much-needed Federal troops from the North's advance on Richmond. It was Robert E. Lee's idea to have Jackson take the offensive in the valley and prevent George B. McClellan from receiving reinforcements for his Peninsula campaign. The eccentric Confederate general faced superior numbers—both Nathaniel Banks' corps, based in Winchester to protect Washington, and John Frémont's force, preparing to invade east Tennessee.

But strengthened by Richard B. Ewell's division, Jackson was ready to move in early May with 17,000 troops, putting his strategy, "Always mystify, mislead, and surprise the enemy," into action. He ordered his equally mystified men east, pretending to head for Richmond, then suddenly put them on trains to return west. Disembarking at Staunton, the Confederates marched through the Alleghenies and smashed Frémont's unsuspecting front guard at the small town of McDowell on May 8. Jackson then scurried back into the valley to confront Banks' force, rumored to be preparing to join McClellan. Aided by intricate maps detailing the tortuous terrain and local scouts and civilian spies reporting the enemy's troop movements, he pressed his infantry north at a grueling pace. After fooling Banks into expecting an attack on his entrenched troops at Strasburg, Jackson swung east and hit one of his small, detached forces at Front Royal on May 23.

Jackson continued north, and with the Union capital now threatened, Banks, who earned his command more through political connections than military prowess, was forced to rush back to his base at Winchester. Outnumbering the Federals more than two to one, the Confederates attacked at dawn on May 25 in a rout that sent the Union troops fleeing 35 miles, all the way back to the Potomac River and into Northern territory. In the process, Jackson's troops netted a treasure trove of food, weapons, and medical supplies.

The Union's panicked leaders assumed the Confederates were preparing to invade. Abraham Lincoln called for a massive convergence on Jackson: Frémont was ordered into the valley from the west, Banks was directed to regroup and hit the Confederate rear from the north, and at Fredericksburg, Irvin McDowell was told to shelve plans to rein-

About 200 of Jackson's soldiers captured in the Shenandoah Valley, May 1862.

force McClellan on the Peninsula and send several additional divisions from the east. Ready with another surprise, Jackson led his army further north toward Harpers Ferry, as if preparing to cross into Maryland, then turned around and began an incredible dash south all the way to the other end of the Shenandoah Valley to evade the approaching forces. He relentlessly drove his troops— already exhausted by the three battles— marching them a punishing 25 miles a day. Their efforts poorly coordinated, Frémont, Banks, and McDowell could not catch the swiftly moving Confederates. Frémont and James Shields, leading one of McDowell's divisions, did manage to follow behind, fighting several rear actions, and when Jackson crossed the Shenandoah River at Port Republic, they had him caught between their two forces.

On June 8, however, the Confederates fought off a poorly mounted assault by Frémont near the small village of Cross Keys, and the next morning, Jackson took the offensive against Shields back at Port Republic, defeating the Federals after a tough three-hour battle. That night, the Confederates withdrew from the valley and boarded trains the following week to join Robert E. Lee's army outside Richmond.

The Shenandoah campaign made Stonewall Jackson a hero throughout the South. It was a legendary strategic triumph: outmaneuvering three armies and winning five straight combat victories, managing in all but one to mount a larger force despite being badly outnumbered overall. And it was a triumph of sheer courage, with Jackson's stalwart infantrymen covering over 350 miles and showing just why they were known as "the Foot Cavalry." Robert E. Lee's purpose was achieved; kept on the run and in the dark, surprised by lightning attacks and defeated in battle, nearly 60,000 Union were held in the Shenandoah Valley during a crucial period when the South was struggling to defend its capital.

Shenandoah Valley Campaign, Sheridan's

AUGUST 7, 1864–MARCH 2, 1865

Ordered to put a decisive stop to Jubal Early's activities near Washington, D.C., Philip Sheridan organized the Army of the Shenandoah and began a seven-month rampage through the fertile Virginia valley, destroying the land as well as Early's forces before he was through. Commanding approximately 40,000 battle-tested cavalry and infantry troops, Sheridan began his advance up the valley in early August.

With reservations both military and political in nature—Lee had recently reinforced Early with infantry, cavalry, and artillery and Lincoln wanted to avoid a major defeat before his election in November—Sheridan's initial advance was quite cautious; he only skirmished with his Confederate enemies during August and early September. In fact, it was not until William Tecumseh Sherman had captured Atlanta on September 2 that Sheridan was encouraged enough in the Union position to take a more aggressive approach. After that, Sheridan attacked mercilessly.

On September 19, his troops met the Confederates on a field near the town of Winchester for a vicious, all-day battle that ended with a Confederate retreat to safe ground at Fisher's Hill. The total losses at the battle of Winchester amounted to more than 8,500 men. Three days later, on September 22, Sheridan sent three divisions under George Crook to attack the Confederate left while he led the remaining Federals on a frontal assault of the Confederate position at Fisher's Hill.

With another Union victory under his belt, Sheridan decided to return to Winchester to reinforce Grant. Early, meanwhile, retreated to Mount Jackson, near the Blue Ridge Mountains. Sheridan grouped his forces at Harrisonburg for a few weeks, then headed back down the valley toward Winchester.

As he withdrew, Sheridan stripped the country of provisions and stock, burned crops, and destroyed property, adhering to the "scorched earth" policy also promulgated by his commander, Sherman. By doing so, he stripped not only the Southerner's land, but their dignity as well. He was so successful in his efforts to devastate the countryside, he

Sheridan and his men moving up the Shenandoah Valley, December 1864.

bragged that "a crow would have had to carry its rations if it had flown across the Valley."

He was furiously pursued by Confederate cavalry, who so harassed his troops that he finally ordered commander Alfred Torbert to "either whip the enemy or get whipped yourself." On October 9, Torbert indeed whipped the Confederate cavalry at Tom's Brook. By the middle of October, the Union army was camped at Cedar Creek, while its commander was traveling to meet with Secretary of War Edwin Stanton in Washington, D.C. It was during Sheridan's absence that Early decided to make another attempt to beat the Army of the Shenandoah.

Launching a surprise attack at dawn on October 19, Early managed to drive the Federals back from several successive positions during the morning and early afternoon. Sheridan made it back to the front in time to rally his retreating forces and deliver a devastating counterattack that essentially crushed Early's army. On March 2, Sheridan and Early met in one futile skirmish that ended in another Confederate defeat at Waynesborough. This engagement marked the end of major military action in the Shenandoah Valley; Early's career was over and Sheridan joined with Grant for the final assault against the Confederates at Appomattox Station.

Sherman's March to the Sea

AUGUST–DECEMBER 1864

Fulfilling his vow to "make Georgia howl," Union General William Tecumseh Sherman brought the brutalities of modern total war to the citizens of the deep South in the final months of 1864. "War is cruelty and you cannot refine it," he told Atlanta's mayor after capturing the city in September and forcing most of its inhabitants to evacuate. And it was precisely Sherman's intention to use that cruelty as a weapon against the Confederacy—to strike against civilians as well as armies and crush the spirit of the people who were supporting and sustaining the South's war effort.

Rather than confront John Bell Hood's forces to the west, Sherman wanted to head southeast, rolling through the heartland of Georgia all the way to Savannah on the Atlantic coast. In the process, his troops would wreck the state's transportation system and keep its bountiful supply of crops from reaching hungry Confederate armies. Though Ulysses S. Grant and Abraham Lincoln were both somewhat skeptical, they approved Sherman's plan.

On November 15, the Army of Georgia and Army of the Tennessee began heading out of Atlanta, burning much of the city before they departed. Marching in two columns, Sherman's 62,000-man force created a front 25 to 60 miles wide and proceeded to destroy bridges, factories, warehouses, and supply depots that lay in their broad path.

Telegraph lines were cut, and miles of railroad track were torn up and twisted around tree trunks to make what the troops called "Sherman's hairpins." Cut off from its own communications and supply lines, the Union army had to live off the land, a task the soldiers undertook with special vigor. Sherman gave them permission to "forage liberally," and while they were told to avoid undue plunder of private property, discipline was lax and the order was mostly overlooked. In the words of one private, the troops "raised Hell." Livestock was confiscated, driven off, or simply slaughtered. Details of foragers known as "bummers" roamed through the fertile countryside daily, carting back wagonloads of meat, vegetables, and grain. The fall harvest was in and the corn that the onetime cotton planters of Georgia had begun growing for the soldiers of the Confederacy now fed the Northern invaders.

While Sherman was depriving Robert E. Lee's army of the goods it so desperately needed to continue waging war, his own troops had far more than they could eat or carry, and simply discarded the rest or distributed it among fugitive slaves. The Union commander, no great believer in emancipation, could not stop nearly 25,000 liberated blacks from following the Northern force on foot or by wagon. There were other followers as well: deserters from both armies, Georgia unionists, and sundry renegades, eager to participate in the pillaging but obeying no one's command.

With Sherman doing little to discourage the marauders, they looted mansions, slave quarters, and churches alike, razing plantations, setting fires to houses and barns, and

Refugees in Georgia trying to outrun Sherman's March to the Sea.

committing other pointless acts of vandalism and destruction. To the citizens of Georgia, however—particularly the women and children who felt the brunt of the mayhem—there was little to distinguish the stragglers from the soldiers, and an understandable hatred of Sherman and the North was spawned that endured for generations. But the Federal troops were in high spirits throughout the march, better fed than they had ever been in their army careers and facing little armed resistance. The opposition was limited to a few thousand state troopers, militiamen, and an outnumbered cavalry corps that Sherman's horsemen easily contained. After annihilating a small force that attacked its rear-guard at Griswoldville on November 22, the Union army captured and ravaged Milledgeville, Georgia's capital, the following day.

Aside from a few brief skirmishes, there were no other confrontations, and the land mines, felled trees, and burnt bridges that the Confederates desperately hoped would slow Sherman's progress were barely an annoyance. Finishing its nearly 300-mile march to the sea on December 10, the Union troops reached the Atlantic coast just below Savannah, having inflicted, by Sherman's own estimation, over $100 million worth of damage.

He prepared to assault the city, but Confederate general William S. Hardee soon withdrew his 10,000-man defense force. Occupying Savannah on December 22, Sherman sent a telegram to Abraham Lincoln two days later, presenting the city to the president "as a Christmas gift." Then, with central Georgia left devastated and the entire South demoralized, the Union general and his troops turned their relentless attention to the Carolinas.

Shiloh, Battle of
APRIL 6–7, 1862

Essentially a tactical draw, this bloodiest engagement of the war to date came to be recognized as an important Union victory, although commanding general Ulysses S. Grant received much criticism for his efforts. In the North, it was initially referred to as the Battle of Pittsburg Landing, after the Tennessee River embankment the Union forces were defending, but both sides came to call the battle by the name of a small Methodist log meetinghouse near where some of the fiercest fighting occurred—a church known as Shiloh, from the Hebrew word for "place of peace."

Grant and his 42,000 troops had been bivouacked on the west side of the Tennessee River near the Mississippi border for almost a month in early spring 1862, waiting for the arrival of Don Carlos Buell's army. Together, the forces were to head south to attack Corinth, a major Southern railroad center. At Corinth, Confederate General Albert Sidney Johnston decided to go on the offensive and catch the Union troops at their encampment before Buell's forces joined them. His second-in-command, Pierre G. T. Beauregard, originally favored the idea, then became convinced that the 22-mile march of over 20,000 soldiers would be detected and wanted to abandon the whole enterprise, certain that Grant would be receiving his reinforcements.

But by the morning of Sunday, April 6, when the Confederates arrived at Pittsburg Landing, there was no sign of Buell, and Johnston's forces surprised Grant, who was away from the front nursing an injured leg. At 8 a.m. the Southern army attacked, overrunning the divisions of Generals William T. Sherman and Benjamin Prentiss near Shiloh Church after three hours of ferocious fighting, with both sides suffering awful casualties. The Confederates' momentum was slowed, however, as ravenous Southern troops started foraging through the abandoned Federal camps to grab a quick breakfast.

As disorganization mounted, both Northern and Southern soldiers—four-fifths of whom had never been in battle before—scrambled to assemble in their correct units. The fighting soon deteriorated into dozens of furious, confused skirmishes; Confederate troops dressed in both blue and gray started firing on each other, and hundreds of infantrymen from both sides fled the battlefield in fear. Medical personnel and ambulance corps were unequipped to handle such overwhelming numbers of dead and wounded. Attention quickly focussed on one sunken road in a dense thicket where a small line of Union soldiers had been ordered by the newly arrived Grant, to hold the position at all costs.

Swarming with shells and bullets, the area

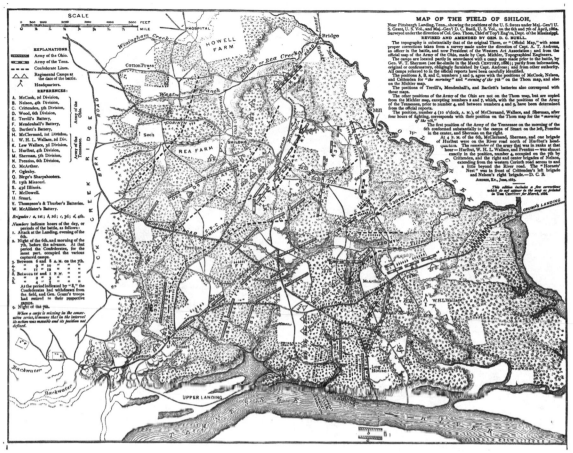

Map of the field of Shiloh.

became known as "the Hornet's Nest," and there the Federals beat back a dozen massive Rebel charges. As he directed the assaults, Confederate commander Johnston was shot in the foot and, with his staff keeping the news from his army, bled to death at 2:30 p.m. Three hours later, under fire from 62 Confederate cannon, the 2,200 defenders of the Hornet's Nest were finally forced to surrender. While the delay gave Grant the chance to amass a line along Pittsburg Landing, supported by two gunboats and heavy artillery,

the day had gone badly for the Union, notwithstanding the Confederates' loss of Johnston. As darkness fell—and with it rain—Beauregard, now commanding the Southern forces, suspended a new assault until the following morning.

That night, however, Don Carlos Buell's Federal reinforcements arrived, and Southern forces awoke to face a Union army nearly twice as large as their own, including 30,000 fresh troops. The fighting resumed at 7:30 a.m. and the Union forces retook almost all

Grant's last line at Shiloh.

the ground they had lost the previous day. Making one counterattack, the Southerners kept falling back until, in the late afternoon, Beauregard ordered a withdrawal back to Corinth. With Nathan Bedford Forrest's aggressive cavalry covering the retreat, the Union army did not pursue.

The Federals could still claim a victory for holding their position, and the battle was indeed a serious setback for the Confederacy's position in the West. But Grant, despite redeeming himself on the battle's second day, was castigated for being caught by

surprise in the first place. Falsely accused—by his superior Henry Halleck, among others—of being drunk in battle, he was also blamed for the huge number of Union deaths. The losses on both sides were appalling. With 13,047 Union and 10,694 Confederate casualties, including a total of nearly 3,500 killed, more than twice the number of soldiers fell at Shiloh than in all the previous engagements of the war combined.

The battle may have affirmed the bravery of Union and Confederate soldiers, but it ended any lingering romance in the North and South about the conflict. And it taught its participants a ghastly lesson. After Shiloh, Grant recollected, "I gave up all hope of saving the Union except by complete conquest."

Snake Creek Gap
MAY 1864, ATLANTA CAMPAIGN

This broad valley in the mountains near Dalton, Georgia, figured several times in the action surrounding the Atlanta campaign, William T. Sherman's extended attempt to take and hold the critical railroad city.

At the beginning of the Federal march, Snake Creek Gap was the initial objective of Union General James McPherson's cavalry; between May 7 and 8 the blue horsemen attempted to swing through the gap as part of a three-pronged attack aimed at turning the left flank of Confederate General Joseph E. Johnston's army. Sixty thousand Southern soldiers held a strongly entrenched position on the ridges above Dalton, extending outward across Sherman's front. On the afternoon of the eighth, McPherson's men made a sally against Snake Creek Gap in hopes that Johnston's men would be too preoccupied repulsing the attacks of Sherman and General George Thomas elsewhere along the line. The Federal cavalry, however, met with only limited success.

The next morning, however, saw heavy fighting everywhere along the contested battle line. After another attempt to cut through Snake Creek Gap and attack the rear of Johnston's line, McPherson decided on the basis of reconnaissance that the Confederates were too well dug in and retired to a safer position, from which he sent to Sherman for further instructions. There is still discussion to this day as to why McPherson, normally a combative opponent, would have made such a decision; certainly at the time it annoyed Sherman.

Throughout the next day, May 10, there were more isolated fights and skirmishes. Johnston adopted a holding stance, knowing that reinforcements under Leonidas K. Polk were on their way from Mississippi. Sherman, on the other hand, was goaded by McPherson's inaction into committing his entire army to a passage through Snake Creek Gap. This action was begun the next day, with Resaca the nearest objective beyond the gap. By the end of the day on May 12, almost all of Sherman's men had made it through Snake Creek Gap and were poised to strike Resaca; Johnston evacuated Dalton that evening and arrayed his forces along Sherman's front, preparing to offer battle. Polk's reinforcements arrived, and the stage was set for the bloody two-day attempt to take or hold Resaca, Georgia.

Spotsylvania, Battle of
MAY 7–19, 1864

Directly on the heels of the bloody Battle of the Wilderness, the armies of Ulysses S. Grant and Robert E. Lee lost thousands more in over a week of equally fierce fighting outside the tiny Virginia crossroads town of Spotsylvania Court House in May 1864. The Federal troops anticipated a retreat following the earlier battle, but instead, Grant ordered them to advance further south. Some contend that he was purposely waging a brutal and costly war of attrition, quite willing to sustain unprecedented Union casualties to wear down the enemy's outnumbered forces. But his actual goal was far more strategic, hoping to force Lee's army into the open, where it could be smashed decisively by the Union's superior numbers and weaponry.

Anticipating Grant's move and not wanting the Federals to block his way to Richmond, Lee and his forces raced south as well and, on May 8, arrived at Spotsylvania first, where they began constructing formidable protective fieldworks. Grant now had to take the offensive and intended to make a showdown of it, proclaiming he would "fight it out on this line if it takes all summer." After an abortive attempt to hit Lee's left flank, he ordered an attack on an arched salient called the "Mule Shoe" near the center of the Confederate line. Supported by heavy artillery fire, a Union division under an intense young colonel, Emory Upton, made a wild, running charge in the late afternoon on May 10, breaking through the enemy's strong defenses and taking 1,000 prisoners before being driven back.

Encouraged by the initial success, Grant decided to mount a larger assault against the Confederate center. At 4:30 a.m. on May 12, Winfield Scott Hancock's 15,000-strong corps led off the attack, breaching the inverted v-shaped Southern line, capturing nearly an entire infantry division, and dividing Lee's army. The Confederates were pushed back almost half a mile while the Federals regrouped in the trenches they had just overrun.

Answering the onslaught, Lee himself prepared to lead a countercharge, but, as they had the week before at the Wilderness, his troops insisted he move to safety in the rear. The two armies then battled for 20 hours straight in some of the most ferocious hand-to-hand combat in the annals of warfare. Soaked in blood and rain, the small piece of land over which they fought—known as "the Bloody Angle" ever after—was soon carpeted with layers of dead and wounded soldiers, while the hail of bullets flying around them sliced down trees nearly two feet thick. Both sides held their ground until well after midnight when Lee finally ordered his exhausted troops to fall back to a new, swiftly dug line of earthworks.

Over the next several days, Grant made unsuccessful attempts in the rain to flank the Confederates, and then, on May 18, tried another frontal assault that merely produced hundreds of new Union casualties. More than 17,500 Union soldiers had been killed, wounded, or captured at Spotsylvania. While the Confederacy's total was significantly smaller—10,000—the losses were far more devastating to the dwindling Southern forces.

Lee's army was hardly finished, however, and on May 19 took the offensive and mounted an assault on Grant's right. Withstanding the attack, Grant finally acknowledged that he could not dislodge and defeat Lee here. The next day, the Army of the Potomac was on the move south once more, with the Army of Northern Virginia scrambling anew to beat them to the next point of confrontation. Again, too locked in conflict to allow the customary period of recuperation following a major battle, both sides would plunge directly into more fighting.

Trevilian Station, Battle of
JUNE 11–12, 1864

In the aftermath of the bloody fighting at Cold Harbor at the beginning of June 1864, General U. S. Grant began maneuvering his army to take the best advantage of successes gained in the fighting around Richmond.

Robert E. Lee sent his cavalry corps to try and prevent the Federal cavalry, under the command of General Philip Sheridan, from joining up with the Union forces under General David Hunter, moving through the Shenandoah Valley. The Confederate cavalry was in a state of some confusion, owing to the death in May of their fabled leader, Jeb Stuart; neither Wade Hampton nor Fitzhugh Lee had yet been named to replace the fallen commander, and the two men, who disliked one another, were not entirely in accord as to how they should move. But they did manage to get their troops into position around Trevilian Station, blocking Sheridan's path.

The fighting was incredibly confused. Sheridan's protégé, General George Custer,

attacked the rear of Hampton's line—but Fitz Lee came to Hampton's rescue. Custer found himself facing his old friend and West Point classmate, General Thomas Rosser, who foiled the attack. Hampton was able to retire in good order, but Lee took the brunt of the attack and was driven back in disarray. During the night, Hampton's men dug in across Sheridan's path, causing the Federal commander to abandon his plan of linking up with Hunter.

The next day, Sheridan repeatedly attacked the entrenchment put up by the Confederates, but it was to no avail. Unable to root out or ride around the men of Hampton and Lee, Sheridan was forced to return the way he had come. The cost was high—slightly over 1,000 of his 8,000 effective troopers were killed, captured or wounded—and the end result was an embarrassing defeat. But the Confederate losses had been costly, too, for of 5,000 men engaged, Hampton and Lee lost more than 600 soldiers—men they could not spare, as Confederate resources continued to dwindle.

Vicksburg, Campaign and Siege of
APRIL–JULY 4, 1863

Abraham Lincoln called the capture of Confederate Vicksburg "the key" to Union victory. By seizing the Mississippi city, the Union would gain control of the Mississippi River, thereby cutting the Confederacy in half

Battery Sherman, just before the Battle of Vicksburg.

and taking its most important supply line. Although the war would drag on for two more years, the death knell for the Confederacy was sounded when the Union plan to win Vicksburg succeeded.

The strategic penetration of the South down the Mississippi started with Ulysses S. Grant's capture of Fort Donelson and Fort Henry early in 1862. In April of the same year, David Farragut had seized New Orleans and, with Nathaniel Banks, took control of the river north almost to the border of Mississippi. The Confederates remained in control of the part of the river that lay adjacent to the southern half of Mississippi, a segment heavily guarded by the strongholds of Vicksburg and Port Hudson.

In the fall of 1862, Ulysses S. Grant was ordered to take Vicksburg and secure the river for the North. The challenge was formidable. Vicksburg was well defended; its strategic importance was not underestimated by the South. Confederate forces under Lieutenant John C. Pemberton, who would be assisted by his commander Joseph E. Johnston, were charged with defending the city. In addition to a strong Confederate military presence, the city was protected by its geographic position. Nearly surrounded by low-lying delta, Vicksburg's location at the mouth of the Yazoo River and the Mississippi made a successful Union approach almost impossible.

During the fall and spring of 1862 to 1863, Grant and his corps commanders, William Tecumseh Sherman, John A. McClernand, and James B. McPherson had made four equally frustrating attempts to penetrate the swamps, bayous, and woods around Vicksburg. Finally, by April 1863, Grant devised a brilliant, albeit risky, plan to take the city. On April 30, with naval support from David Dixon Porter, he and his troops traveled by ship across from the west bank of the Mississippi to Grand Gulf on the east bank south of Vicksburg. From here, he would launch an infantry attack on the city.

The key to the success of Grant's plan lay in keeping the two Confederate forces—Pemberton's at Vicksburg and reinforcements soon to be commanded by Johnston about 45 miles to the east at Jackson—from combining. Grant decided to turn first against Jackson. By attacking and defeating that force, he could concentrate on Vicksburg without fear of a threat to his northern flank or rear. By the time Confederate General Johnston arrived at Jackson on May 13, he saw the impossibility of holding the city. He had just 6,000 men to oppose the approximately 25,000-man Union army. Johnston evacuated the city, freeing Grant to concentrate on Vicksburg. Leaving Sherman with two divisions to finish destroying the supply and communication lines at Jackson, Grant ordered McClernand to march westward, roughly following the route of the Southern Mississippi Railroad.

In the meantime, confusion and miscalcu-

lation reigned within the Confederate army. Although ordered by Johnston to move northwest to reunite the two forces, Pemberton instead chose to attempt an attack on Grant's line of communications to the south. On May 13, his advance stalled due to drenching rain and flood waters. While waiting for a bridge across the swollen Baker's Creek to be completed, he received another directive from Johnston to move north. This time he complied and countermarched.

Meanwhile, Johnston, north of Jackson, moved further away to avoid a perceived threat from Sherman. By May 16, Pemberton was essentially trapped. McPherson and McClernand's corps were rapidly closing in from the west, and Grant moved toward Vicksburg from the east. Pemberton deployed his three divisions of about 22,000 men at Champion's Hill, a prominent knoll covered with woods east of Vicksburg. McClernand arrived at about 6:00 a.m. and McPherson a few hours later; between them they had about 29,000 men. The ensuing battle was a bitter, day-long event in which more than 6,000 men were killed. Forced to withdraw, Pemberton attempted to delay the pursuing Federals by destroying the bridges across the Big Black River. The Union simply rebuilt the bridges and continued their pursuit, engaging the Confederates in another battle at the river which lost the Rebels another 1,700 men.

By May 18, Pemberton and about 32,000 men were trapped behind the defenses of Vicksburg. The next day, all of Grant's forces, about 45,000 men, had closed in. Grant hoped to capitalize on the demoralized state of the

Confederate defenders by launching a frontal assault on the city. The attack began at 2:00 p.m. and raged for hours; the Confederates were far more tenacious and stubborn than Grant had anticipated. When a similar approach failed on May 22, Grant settled his troops in for what he knew would be a long and arduous siege.

Standard siege works were quickly constructed and mines were planted. The opposing trenches grew so close that hand grenades could be thrown and then returned before the devices exploded. Constant shelling and the growing shortage of rations made Pemberton's plight more hopeless each day. Sickness and wounds had rendered about 50 percent of his men unfit for active service. Civilians also suffered from the unceasing bombardment and shortage of food. "We are utterly cut off from the world," wrote one resident, "surrounded by a circle of fire. . . . The fiery shower of shells goes on, day and night . . . People do nothing but eat what they can get, sleep when they can, and dodge the shells."

Finally, six weeks after Pemberton had withdrawn into Vicksburg, he was ready to relinquish the city. The opposing commanders met on July 2 to discuss terms of surrender; hoping to gain paroles for his men, Pemberton agreed to surrender on Independence Day. Thirty-one thousand Confederates surrendered on July 4, 1863, and the Stars and Stripes was raised above the Vicksburg Court House. Coming the day after the Federal victory at Gettysburg, the fall of Vicksburg marked the beginning of the end of the Confederacy.

★   ★   ★

Wilderness, Battle of the
MAY 5–6, 1864

The first battlefield confrontation between Ulysses S. Grant and Robert E. Lee, this engagement in Virginia's Rapidan basin marked the beginning of a 40-day campaign that included some of the bloodiest fighting of the Civil War. Grant, who had been appointed the Union's general-in-chief two months earlier, intended nothing less than a showdown between Meade's Army of the Potomac and Lee's Army of Northern Virginia that, together with coordinated efforts by other Federal forces elsewhere, would bring about the Confederacy's defeat by the end of the year.

On May 4, Union troops began crossing the Rapidan River and marching south to face the Confederates, returning to the location of the Battle of Chancellorsville. Grant had hoped his troops could avoid a clash with the enemy until they passed the notorious dense forest of trees and shrubs known as "the Wilderness." Choked with heavy underbrush and still littered with human bones and other battle debris, this was the spot where Lee's army achieved such devastating success exactly one year earlier.

The Confederate general relied on the Wilderness once again, reckoning that the Union army's great numerical advantage— 115,000 to his force of 60,000—would be offset by the difficult terrain. The battle began early on the morning of May 5, when Union and Confederate troops stumbled upon each other as the Federals attempted to cross the forest. Both sides received reinforcements, and

The Battle of the Wilderness, May 5 and 6, 1864.

by 1 p.m., the Union mounted a major assault. With the troops soon swallowed up in the impenetrable thickets, however, the fighting plunged into total chaos. Visibility was less than 50 yards, hampered even further by the smoke of battle and brushfires ignited by bursting shells. Having few discernible targets, many soldiers just shot blindly into the woods, sometimes hitting their own men, while entire units got lost in the tangled undergrowth, forcing their commanders to resort to compasses to find their way.

As Lee anticipated, the terrain did even the odds. With far fewer experienced woodsmen among the Northern troops, the superior size of the Union force created more of a logistical problem than a tactical advantage. But the greater numbers did allow the Federals to absorb greater casualties. Commanded by the resolute Grant, they continued making relentless assaults, repulsed each time by Confederate counterattacks. By the end of the first day's fighting, Grant managed to weaken Lee's right flank, and was positioned for attack.

At dawn on May 6, Union forces began slamming through the Confederate center, advancing almost a mile, nearly all the way to Lee's field headquarters. By this time, however, much-needed Confederate reinforcements from James Longstreet's corps were beginning to arrive on the field. Hood's Texas Brigades, the celebrated infantry unit now actually under John Gregg, was soon poised for a counterattack. Lee himself intended to lead the charge, but the Texas troops refused to begin their assault until the Confederate commander was safely behind the lines.

Throughout the morning, Longstreet's fresh troops pushed the flustered Union men back. Following an unfinished railroad line all but hidden under bushes and vines, the Confederates had a makeshift pathway for a massive attack on the Union's left flank. Their momentum was crushed, though, when Longstreet was accidentally shot and wounded by his own troops. By the time Lee mounted a new assault in the late afternoon, Union forces had regrouped and were able to hold their position.

Meanwhile, in a late attack on the Union's right, Confederate John B. Gordon drove Federal troops back one mile, although they managed to regain most of the ground by nightfall. Still, the setback caused great alarm at Grant's headquarters. While the Union commander kept his composure, even chastising his gloomy aides for bemoaning Lee's supposed superior prowess, some eyewitnesses reported that Grant himself broke down in tears when he retired to his tent.

Both commanders had good reason to be upset. The two-day battle cost the Union army 17,500 casualties to the Confederates' 7,750, with neither side gaining much ground. At several points, the fighting had to be halted while both sides attempted to rescue wounded comrades being burned alive by the uncontrolled brushfires raging through the Wilderness. The following day, however, as the two armies began skirmishing, Grant did not call for the expected retreat. To the contrary,

notwithstanding his far heavier losses and a tactical draw on the battlefield, he ordered an advance.

Intent on keeping his promise to Abraham Lincoln that "whatever happens, there will be no turning back," Grant's plan now was for George Meade's army to move further south—past Lee's right—and position itself provocatively between the Confederate forces and their capital, Richmond. The fighting would resume within days, 12 miles away at the strategic crossroads town of Spotsylvania Court House.

Wilson's Creek, Battle of
AUGUST 10, 1861

The second military engagement of the war after First Bull Run was a small but vicious battle over the future of the border state Missouri. The commander of Federal forces was Nathaniel Lyon, who had amassed some 5,500 troops at Springfield, Missouri. The Confederate army of about 10,000 men advanced on Springfield at the beginning of August, finally camping at Wilson's Creek about 15 miles away. Aware of the enemy position, Lyon planned a surprise attack. He would divide his forces, sending Colonel Franz Sigel to attack from the south while he himself led a frontal attack on the main body from the north. Although his strategy was sound, Lyon was outnumbered more than two to one, and the soldiers he did command had almost no battlefield experience.

The resulting battle was a bitter, confused hand-to-hand struggle. It began at about 4 a.m., when the Northern column moved out and drove back the Confederate outposts from the west side of the creek. A flank guard broke away to move against a Confederate force on the east side and was able to drive it back as well. Sigel, however, was having difficulty advancing from the south. At 5:30 a.m., he attacked the Confederate cavalry, then took an intermediate position and regrouped. Troops under Louis Hébert and cavalry under Thomas Churchill managed to send Sigel's poorly trained troops into confused retreat, leaving Lyon's men vulnerable.

However, Lyon's troops were positioned on an incline called Oak Hill, from which they had already repulsed two charges by 10:30 a.m. Lyon himself had been wounded twice, in the head and leg, but stayed alive long enough to rally his troops for yet another defense of the position. After another hour of brutal fighting, the Confederates broke off action and withdrew down the hill.

Samuel Sturgis, who had assumed command after Lyon's death, ordered his exhausted army to retreat to Springfield, thereby making one of the most bitterly contested withdrawals of the war. Had Sturgis pressed the battle, the fight over Missouri might have been won that day. Instead, the state would be the site of bitter fighting throughout the rest of the war.

★　★　★